My Miracle Experiences

By Richard Langner

DORRANCE
PUBLISHING CO
EST. 1920
PITTSBURGH, PENNSYLVANIA 15238

Dorrance Publishing Co
585 Alpha Drive
Pittsburgh, PA 15238
Visit our website at www.dorrancebookstore.com

ISBN: 979-8-8852-7139-4
eISBN: 979-8-8852-7866-9

Richard Langner – Biography

Entrepreneur, inventor, businessman, author, and politician. At the end of June 2016, I flew helicopters and I had been escorted by two F-16s, fully armed, from New York City to Roosevelt Aircraft Carrier of Virginia Coast to debate problems at South China Sea. In five minutes I put my plans on the table, which were immediately approved by all debaters: President Putin, President Holland, and Chancellor Angela Markel. President Obama was present but was only sitting and listening while I debated.

At the end of October 2016 I hosted a press conference with presidential candidates DJT and HRC at T Tower.

Richard Langner was born on March 6, 1947, in Koscian in Poland and has been living in the United States of America since March 27, 1971. Net worth today is more than three trillion. Spouse: Anna Langner (m 1977–present).

Preface

All these stories in my book are true. They are in the archives or proved by cameras. Today, cameras are installed everywhere. The Lord came here with an army of angels to protect me and to prepare me for something big. Just like on January 17, 2016, at the Red Tail Lodge, when I entered the press conference room, the Lord Himself yelled, "Stop the music. Here comes the King! He is the new King." Then came another group; they call themselves devils. Also, they told me that they are angels too. Maybe they are; they are doing their jobs they were ordered to do. They were trying to pull me on their side, by destroying me, making me weak. One of them told me in 2012, "We came here to destroy you in every possible way." From the beginning they were very successful. But little by little, I learned from them, that they are afraid of me. I learned how to fight them back, and I'm doing this to this day.

In 2007 I did start trading stocks on the internet. I had been buying stocks on the internet, and I sold them the same way. Sometimes the next day, sometimes I held them a little longer, and then when I thought it was time to sell them, I sold them on the internet.

In the summer of 2007, I made plans to sell a huge amount of solar stocks. They went up, after they had a good report. That's why I made my decision to sell and make a good profit.

Those around me always know what I think; they knew my plans. The leader was connected to my brain. (People committing sins by their physical acts also by saying and bad thinking, so guardian angels know also what people think.)

They couldn't let this happen. They came here to destroy me every possible way. On that summer day, I got up early in the morning. I did my usual thing I'm doing every morning. After my breakfast, I went to the computer to check my stocks, which overnight went up a lot, which made me very happy. I just couldn't wait till the stock market opened. Many times I sold my stocks after the market just opened.

That day was beautiful weather, full sun, blue sky; there wasn't even one tiny cloud in the sky. I prepared myself to trade; the time was around ten a.m. I heard lightning. After that lightning, the power went off. I stepped outside. I looked up to the sky, and I didn't see a single tiny cloud. That single lightning struck a power transformer, and we were without power for many hours. I couldn't sell my stocks that day. Later that day, the sale was off, and my stocks went down. I had been waiting over a month for another good day to trade my stocks. There were all different situations on days I wanted to trade, like the computer didn't want to open, windows were shut down, and on and on. I was not supposed to make money. They came here to destroy me. Who has that kind of power, to create lightning, and direct it into the spot he or she wanted? Just like moving me from Vernon, New Jersey, to Vatican City in no time. Not too many people have that kind of power.

In 2018 I did start to write all my experiences in the book, wasn't easy because I'm not a writer, but I'm stubborn. I had been born that way; our God created me that way.

In the spring of 2019, I signed a contract with Dorrance Publishing Co. They appointed me a Writing Coach Coordinator, a great one with a lot of passion. Her name was Melissa. I had been working with her for two and a half years. Before her, I had two Writing Coach Coordinators. For some reason, they quit. I thought to myself, They could be threatened by the one who went to Meagan Fox and told her if she would write the book with me, they would destroy her. I believe he went to Melissa and threatened her too, but she was tough, and together, we did finish the manuscript.

On December 7, 2021, I signed a contract with Dorrance Publishing Co., a contract to publish my book.

Now they have the manuscript and are making it into a book. Dorrance Publishing Co. appointed the best coordinators and then editors to work on this project. Each time they thought they did a good job with that manuscript, and after, they mailed it to me. I discovered there were stories mixed up, misspellings, parts of some stories missed. I corrected all that and I mailed it back to my Project Coordinator for correction. Now the editor is working on it, and he can't get it done. The editor has been working on the project for a whole year. They send that manuscript to me for final approval about six times. Now they are still working on it. The last time I did mail that manuscript to the editor was in November. There were only a few corrections. I know who is messing up, those who came here to destroy me, because I won't work with them. They have many reasons to not let me publish this book. They just don't want me to publish all those true stories I wrote in this book.

I believe they are going to manipulate it with this book to the end. If you are reading this book and find some discrepancies, that's not done by me, project coordinator, or editor. That would be done by invisible evils. That would only prove what I wrote in my book is true.

Dorrance Publishing Co. has been trusted by authors for one hundred years. The company has the best qualified employees and they wouldn't make any discrepancies or errors.

I would like to share my true, untold experiences with people of the world.

On November 12, 2012, while eating lunch at my office, I was looking through the window facing Route 23 when I turned my head to the left. I noticed a woman was standing about three feet away from me and I said to her, "How did you get here? The door is locked."

She said, "It's locked; go check." I didn't move. She repeated, "It's locked; go check." I didn't move again; I was afraid of getting up and leaving the room. Strangely enough, I didn't want this woman to leave—even though I had no idea who she was or where she had come from. She noticed my hesitation. Again, she said, "Go, go, go." I got up and I checked, and the door was locked.

That day was very cold, but this woman was wearing a white dress with short sleeves. She had no shoes on her feet and her face was foggy; I couldn't see it clearly. I asked her, "Are you not cold?" She said she didn't have blood. I said, "I have a clean fleece jacket and I can give it to you." She said, "I do not need your jacket; I am not cold."

Then she asked me, "You don't want to live anymore?" I wondered at how she knew that, but I decided to answer her. Something about her seemed ethereal.

I said, "I lost a lot of money on the stock market. The auto business is finished. I have been buying new or couple-years-old total loss cars at auto insurance auctions. After I rebuild them, I sell those cars on eBay. That was great business—what I had been doing for thirty years. Computers destroyed this kind of business. People from all around the world were betting on computers, and we couldn't compete with Africa, South America, China, and Eastern Europe."

WINDOW

INTERIOR SUBJECT PHOTOGRAPHS

On November 12, 2012 angel was standing where that white dot is

She said, "We came here to destroy you because you won't work with us, but we misjudged you. You will get a big house and lots of money." I was startled at that; I still had no idea who this woman was, or where she had come from, or why she had come to destroy me. But I was curious about her prediction.

I asked her, "When?" She said, "Very soon." Then she said, "I have to go." I asked her to stay but she said she must go then. I asked her if she could come back tomorrow, and she told me that one day she will be back.

They were destroying me and my family in every possible way. She, specifically, damaged my car, broke windows in our garage and the door locks after I said I was going to sell my garage to my son for one dollar.

The Lord said something was wrong. I don't want to write that word. He is not who you think he is. Why were they doing that? Because they were living there in my garage. That was their home, which they were protecting every possible way. They came here in 2002. Then my guardian angel said, "We misjudged you. You will get back what you lost."

When we were talking, she told me, "Look for the house and they will pay for it." I had been on the Trulia website looking for houses in Sparta, NJ, and my guardian angel must have known that. She made it sound like all would be well, once I found the house I wanted to buy—like someone else would purchase the house. So, I kept going.

November 12, 2012

I was very confused about what had happened. It felt like an angel had visited me. But because I did not understand who she was or what had happened, I continued to live my life as usual. At that time, my shop was on the market for sale, but this woman came to me again and told me I couldn't sell the garage because that was her home. When she left, she went up with a loud sound. She was also the mother of our daughter, Sophia, who was, at this time, two years old. Now, eight years later, she is close to ten years old.

In November 2012 I had been at the farmer's market. She had nothing in her hands, but she came very close to me, still smiling, and stood in front of me for a few seconds, turned around, and she went outside. That was in November of 2012. Later, I found out from the leader of guardian angels that she was the number two guardian angel. The Lord came here with army of angels to do a special job. I assume to prepare me for something big. An average person won't get this. It's easy for me to talk with Cardinal D because he met with my organizer many times, who is from above, in heaven, and that there was competition for the number-one spot.

April 4, 2013

In Aruba, I was walking on the beach and noticed a young Black woman walking toward me. She was wearing long slacks and a long burgundy wool winter coat over them. She was chic and lovely. In her hand, she was carrying a hat. When she got closer to me, she asked me to wash the sand off her hat, which I did. I couldn't be happier to help her. After she left, I thought to myself, Who could that woman be? She was elegant and smart, but by the way she was dressed, I came to the conclusion that she was an angel and was testing me to see if I'm racist.

I was at Rio Palace in Aruba. Sophia's mother, who was this strange woman, came to our bed when I was sleeping with my wife. She was talking to me and I said to her, "Be quiet!" She said, "Nobody is going to hear us." After a while, she was gone.

Spring of 2013

After, I rebuilt the 2012 Lexus RX-350 truck, which was a total loss; that was a big job. After I painted and finished polishing, I took that nice black Lexus outside to wash and clean it up. When I had been done, I drove it to the showroom. While driving this Lexus, I passed a 2004 Lexus my wife parked in the morning in front of the showroom. In that moment I was passing that car, someone grabbed the steering wheel and was steering toward that parked car.

I had been struggling and I avoided a head-on hit, but the side of that truck was a little damaged. I was very upset; I knew who did that. That was the one who on November 12, 2012, told me she would come here and destroy me because I wouldn't work with them. The next day I got up from bed early after what happened the previous day. I couldn't sleep well. I repaired the small damage. After that I heard Invisible saying to someone that I damaged his car, but he came in and fixed that damage. This was no conversation.

Photograph 10 - A view of the property's frontage along Route 23 as seen from the southwest corner of the property looking in a northerly direction.

Photograph 11 - A view of the front building elevation as seen from the southwest corner of the property looking in a northeasterly direction.

A view of the parking lot at the northern end of the subject property as seen from the west side of Route 23 looking in a northeasterly direction.

On November 12, 2012, my guardian angel told me this is her house, and I can't sell it. Many miracles happened in this building.

At first I didn't hear anything. The next day I parked cars far away from the doors. I was pulling out from the showroom a 2012 Lexus RX-350. Once I passed the showroom door, someone grabbed my steering wheel and stepped on the gas pedal and started driving towards the cars parked outside the garage. This is bad!

I stepped on the brake pedal, and I had been struggling with my steering wheel. But that Invisible was able to steer that 2012 Lexus toward that 2004 Lexus parked outside and damage the fender of that car and the car I was pulling out from the showroom. The car I was pulling from the showroom had left-side bumper corner damage. That was evil's job. When there are good angels, there are also bad ones. When people go to the army, the first few months they are going through tough training to break them down and to teach them discipline.

That was really bad. For the first time in my whole life, I was frightened. From that moment I didn't feel safe at my own place. I didn't know with whom I was dealing. Who they were, what they wanted from me, what I should do next, who I should see. Priest, Cardinal, police, or write to the Pope? I had been thinking about how to stop them.

From that day I had always had on my mind what they would do next. I still have this on my mind. But after many years of dealing with them, I learned a lot. Little by little, I learned from them that they are afraid of me because I have all the power; I'm the one who can end this world. Just do a very simple thing. I know that from them. Also, they said that to the Cardinal and asked him not to do what I asked him to do. But I don't need anybody's help. That's why they were trying to destroy and scare me. But that didn't work well for them, and it's still not working the way they wanted.

Summer 2013

Late Spring–Early Summer. While checking properties through different real estate agencies, I noticed that the owner of one agency looked like my angel. I believed this was a sign. I made an appointment, and the agent took me to a new development, Fox Run, in Sparta. The builder's name was Brian D. I liked that community. Those houses that he built came with nice floorplans. But I felt like, for some reason, this wasn't the place for me. I believe my guardian angel was trying to push me away from this place, so I didn't buy any properties there.

In the summer of 2013, I was on the phone with B.D. and he shocked me by telling me that I had a daughter. Her name was Sophia and she was two and a half years old. Her mother was his sister, who was my guardian angel. Her name was Sheryl. The owner of the real estate agency was Donna, and she was the sister of my guardian angel. Sophia was raised by her family in Vernon, NJ. Sophia is a beautiful girl, and now close to ten years old.

On August 13, 2013 I had been sitting on that wall and I have been talking with the lady from my bank, while my conversation with her I had been pushed of that wall, by my guardian Angel.

On August 13, 2013, I had been sitting on the wall that was between my parking lot and my neighbor's property. The wall on my side was about five feet high. On my neighbor's side it was about two and a half feet high. My feet were on my neighbor's side and my back was toward my parking. I had been talking to my neighbor and with a young lady from the bank about what business I had been doing for a very long time and we liked each other. Many times when I had been at the bank, she asked me to come to her desk and she would take care of my business.

The lady from that bank told me that she lives at the same resort where I'm living. I said to her, "Maybe one day we can go out together."

9

She said, "Yes, we have to." The next thing I know, I was lying in the parking lot, my head was cut, and I was bleeding badly. I'm not entirely sure what happened, but I was frightened.

My neighbor called 911, and a few minutes later, an ambulance arrived. Nurse Linda got out and was ready to put me inside the ambulance, but a blond woman showed up and said, "No, you are not going to take him. We are taking him to Morristown Trauma Center."

The nurse said, "It will take more than an hour to drive there."

The blond woman was my guardian angel, Sophia's mother. She was the one who came to my office on November 12, 2012.

The blond woman replied, "We will take him there by helicopter."

Nurse Linda said, "Do you know how long you have to wait for a helicopter?"

The blond lady said, "It will be quick."

Then the nurse asked her, "Do you know how much it will cost?"

The blond lady said, "Doesn't matter."

Nurse Linda Kelly asked, "Who is he? Is he that important?"

The blond lady answered, "He is very important."

A few minutes later, a helicopter landed across Route 23 on a school parking lot. The ambulance took me to the helicopter, and I was on the way to Morristown. On the helicopter, I was talking to an angel pilot and a blond angel. The blond angel told me, "You have a child, Sophia, to raise." She was jealous because I wanted to go out with that young woman from my bank and she's also my neighbor; that's why she pushed me off the wall. She committed the crimes." I couldn't believe that someone would be so jealous as to push me off a wall. But my guardian angels were always watching over me, making sure no harm would come to me. My angel pilot originally came to work at Vernon

Police Department to protect me better. Mike, the police officer, mentioned that he always knew what was going on.

They rented that helicopter and I was talking with Nurse Linda about that incident; she said she knew something was not right—the helicopter came too soon. She knew there had to be something supernatural and special about me; the helicopter was there so fast that I had to be a very important person in the universe. I told her why I was so important and why I was performing miracles. I also would talk to Nurse Linda after I would eventually bring a man back to life on January 13, 2016, in St. Clair's hospital in Sussex, NJ, as well.

A couple of months later, I was talking to Sophia's mother and she told me that was an angel who was testing me. Sophia's mother was so helpful during this part of my life; I spoke to her frequently about the strange woman who was visiting me. She helped me figure out what was happening and helped me through the tests the angel laid for me.

Winter 2013
In the winter of 2013, I was home by myself when Sophia's mother entered by bedroom. She asked if she could touch my face and I said yes. She touched my face; that's all. I said to her, "Your hands are warm."

She said, "Yes, they are warm." Being surrounded by the energy of the guardian angels was a powerful thing. They learned more about my life and about me, and I learned more about their past.

2014
In 2014, one of my guardian angels told me Sophia's mother doesn't have anything to lose, so sometimes, they are a little reckless. Once, the Lord told me that if those two guardian angels were sent back, I would be the King— the New King.

Also, God gave me the option: I can move out of Sussex County, the state, or the country. My angels told me that. And they would have to go back. That's why they came up with the idea to destroy me in 2012, so that I would be broke and stay in Sussex County. That was then. Now I have things under control.

And now I was seeing her again, in my home, where we said hello to each other. She told me, "You don't know who you are. God is very old, and he will need your help." I was shocked. Of course, anyone would be shocked to hear that God needed his or her help. Anyone would be shocked to be visited by a guardian angel. Today, I do understand my position. I experienced so many things—miracles.

That evening, we talked about many things. I asked her if she wanted to eat, and she said she wasn't allowed to eat here. I supposed it had something to do with her being from heaven. So I asked her when she died, and she told me when she was fourteen years old, she died of disease.

I finished my dinner, had a couple of glasses of red wine, and she just disappeared. Later, the Lord asked me why I was drinking red wine, and I told Him a lot of people drink red wine. He said that drinking red wine is just drinking his blood. After he told me that, I stopped drinking red wine; I'm only drinking white.

Spring 2014
In the spring of 2014, I healed my next-door neighbor, Mark. He was a heavy alcohol drinker, and it completely destroyed his liver. He was waiting for an emergency transplant, and had been waiting for a transplant since I first knew him. I became close friends with Mark, and I wanted to do something to help him, so I decided to heal him.

On June 4, 2014, I had been walking to the lake, the Lord was coming down from the lake and we met on this ski slope where that 'X' is.

I'm living in bear country, and we see them almost every day.
They are all over our neighborhood.

After I healed him, four months later he was painting rooms again. He healed very quickly, and I was so thrilled to see him back to work. It was clear that I still had the power to perform miracles, and that the Lord would still need me on earth to perform good works and miracles.

June 4, 2014

Then, on June 4, 2014, I met the Lord on a ski slope in Vernon, NJ, and talked to him. At that time, I didn't know he was the Lord, but before this meeting, I had seen him many times in different locations in Vernon. I couldn't believe that I had passed him so many times before and didn't recognize him as the Lord. I suppose the Lord makes himself visible to me when he so chooses.

I had never seen anyone like that before. He was tall, about 6'3" to 6'5", and he was wearing khaki pants and a shirt. On his head he had a cup hat, of the same color, in his right hand, and he was holding a long walking stick that wasn't straight. He looked like a shepherd. His face was long, and he had a semi-long black beard. His skin color was sort of light olive. He truly looked unlike anyone I had ever seen before. Even though I was shocked by his appearance, I was not afraid. I felt comforted by his presence.

The day that I met the Lord for the first time was a nice and sunny day. I decided to walk to the lake at our resort, but never before did I start from the bottom of the slope. First, I went to the store to buy myself a drink. I had a backpack on my back, so I prepared myself well, since it was so hot. Once I got on the small hill, I saw a mysterious man walking straight toward me. I said to myself, This time, I'm going to stop him.

When we got closer to each other, we both stopped. I said hello and he said hello. I asked him, "Which way is the lake?" but he didn't say anything. He just turned 180 degrees, and with his whole arm, he pointed to the direction of the lake. His left hand was holding a small branch and I asked him what it was, but he didn't say anything; he just lifted it up and shook it. It was an olive branch with olives—a branch of peace. At this point I knew that this was the Lord, and that he wanted to meet with me.

Summer 2014

Another test of my faith, in the form of a miracle, came in the summer of 2014. I had been walking to the lake at our resort, which was about a forty-five-minute walk away from my condominium. It's a nicely sized lake with a beach, kayaks, and boats. That lake is only for people who live there. On my way back, I heard a woman's voice behind me saying, "A bear is chasing you. Don't panic; it will kill you. Shoot him with your finger."

I turned around, and right behind me there was a big bear running toward me. I lifted my arm up and made my hand like a pistol and I shot him. He made a right turn and ran into the woods with a sound like he was hit. I repeated my action, and the bear made another sound like he was hit and ran away. I couldn't believe what had happened.

The woman next to me said, "Save your energy because you only have so much." I didn't see any woman; that was my guardian angel. Then the Lord appeared, and He and the guardian angels told me I have a taser in my body to protect myself. Once, the Lord told me the priest from my Church was afraid of me because I gave him an electric shock. I didn't give him one. He probably got to believe what I told him what's going on in his Church. Sophia's mother at that time was my guardian angel, and I saw her everywhere. I didn't know that I gave the priest an electric shock. Someone made me do so without me knowing. He, Father, was the head of the Church. After I told him about the miracles at his Church, his duty was to report that to the bishop of Paterson. He was punished and later removed.

The Cardinal of New York told me that father was afraid he would lose his job for some reason. I assume, one day, something is going to happen with this Church. The Cardinal has a picture of me praying with St. Pope John Paul II. They enlarged the picture and clearly recognize him. Also, they have me on film praying with Lord Jesus Christ. But no one knows him the way he looks today. He doesn't look the same as he did over two thousand years ago. Even if he would look like that, people still would be skeptical. Only miracles can prove something. I have more than enough.

Four people have told me that when they sit next to me, they feel electric waves flowing from me and then feel good afterwards. My sister-in-law loves to sit next to me because it makes her feel healthy; I believe she feels the electric waves coming off my body. Not long ago I had been talking to my brother who lives in Poland, and he said that when I was in Poland in 1995, his sister-in-law told him she was feeling electric waves from me and she knew I was different.

On October 29th, 2014, in this dining room O heard invisible talking, and lights in that chandelier had been blinking. I have been sitting in that armchair.

September 10, 2014

On September 10, 2014, my guardian angel came to my condominium, and she told me about my future. I was home by myself because my wife was watching our grandson, who at the time was twenty-six months old. It was late in the afternoon and I was making dinner for myself—porkchops—when at one point I noticed a young woman standing next to me. She was wearing a short skirt and blouse and had very long hair, and she was very nice. I was happy to see her again. I realized that I had met her many times before. I had a conversation with her. The first time I met her was at the farmer's market. I had been picking rolls, and I saw a young woman who was walking towards me, smiling. She had nothing in her hands; she came very close to me, still smiling, stood in front of me for a few seconds, and turned around, and she went outside.

October 29, 2014

I would like to present and share with readers my experiences what happened on that night and how we here on earth are connected with people on the other side—above us. People who died and are living above us. My daughter, Angela Langner, was living with her son, Preston John Sinchera. Sinchera is the last name of her former husband in Mahwah, New Jersey. Mahwah is located in the northeast of New Jersey in Bergen County. In October of 2014 she was working in a hospital in Basking Ridge, New Jersey, as a registered dietitian and nutritionist working with cancer patients. When she was at work, my wife, Anna Langner, was caring for our grandson. We were living in Vernon, New Jersey, in Sussex County, which is located about fifty minutes away from Mahwah. Many times I drove with my wife to watch Preston, our grandson.

On October 29, 2014, my wife drove to watch Preston, but this time by herself. Something told me to stay home. Maybe because she was supposed to sleep over. That's why that night I was at home by myself. Our kitchen, dining room, and family room were all open. That night, around nine o'clock, I was in the family room watching television, a few feet away from the dining room table. At one point I heard people talking in our dining room, a few feet away from me. I did not see anyone. On top of this, the lights started blinking in our chandelier. I don't remember how I started talking with them. Those people were invisible. Finally, one of them asked me to donate this condominium and our shop, I believe, to Heaven's Kingdom.

He asked me to meet him at the Mountain Resort Properties Real Estate Agency at our community, which is located about four hundred yards from our condominium, to sign the deed over to them. I knew some of them personally then. When he said that, I was shocked from what I just heard. I had known some of them since November 12, 2012. But this time they were trying legally to steal our properties. I asked him where I was going to live, and he replied something like this, "We will take you there." I believe he meant they would take me to Heaven. If they would, that would be the end of the world.

Then I asked him what about my wife, and his answer was, "She will go there." I assumed he meant to our daughter. I told him I could sell it to him, and he replied that he couldn't pay for it.

After that I said to him, "Then we have no deal without money." He passed that to someone, somewhere, saying that I said without money there's no deal. I'm one hundred percent sure that was the Lord's negotiator. He had a heavy Russian accent. Later, on January 17, 2016, at Red Tail Lodge, he and I negotiated with powerful world leader. On that day I recognized his voice.

In October 2016, then-candidate President DT made an announcement that he gave a condominium to Richard Langner, at 721 5th Ave, in New York City. He added that his daughter was decorating it. At the end of May 2017, in my kitchen, the Lord and my guardian angel were standing next to me. They were invisible and we were talking about different things. The Lord said to me that I shouldn't complain because "they are good people; they gave you that condominium."

I quickly asked him, "Where is it, where is it?"

The Lord didn't say anything; he was silent. Oops, he bit his tongue. After, he gave me that condominium, the negotiator was doing the paperwork, and since then, they have been holding my deed and key for that unit. On January 20, 2017, at the Oval Office, he said to me that the condominium was in my name. She said, "In a few days, I am going to ask my attorney to go to cityhall to get a duplicate of the deed."

As you can see, some of them are not really that good saints.

Once, Lord said to me, "I would like to live in Manhattan." The Lord is not going to live in Manhattan, New York. On July 26, 2020, Rev. S. read a letter at the end of Mass, which read, "Sell what you have and donate that money to Heaven's Kingdom." Also, that was on St. Francis De Sales's website.

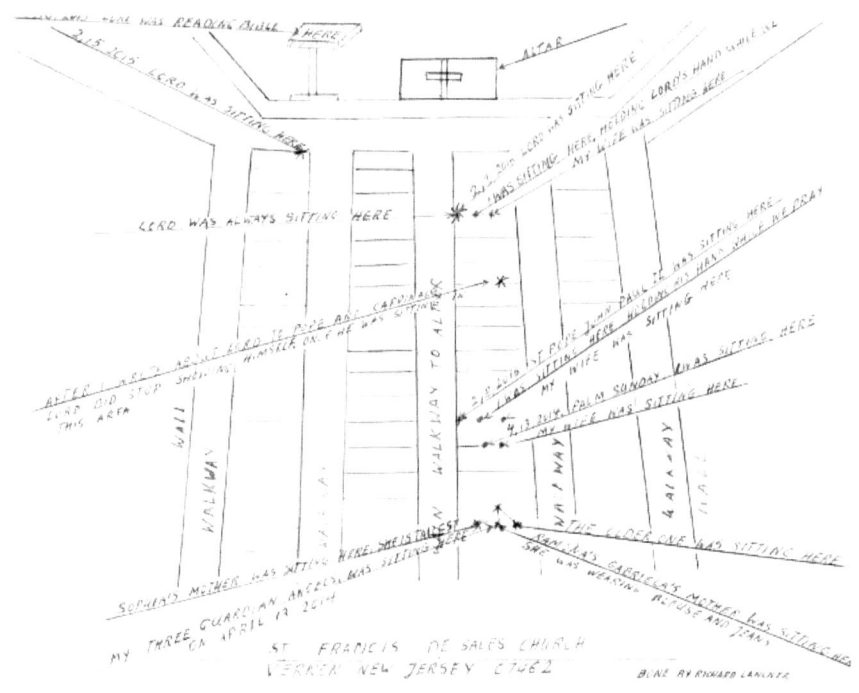

St Francis De Sales Church, Vernon New Jersey 07462

October 29, 2014. That night, around nine o'clock, I was sitting in that armchair, when the action started.

That's good, everything can be done. I'm doing everything I can for our God. But I have to know that's what I'm doing. I'm doing it for Heaven's Kingdom, not for evil's. Because I had very bad experiences with some of them.

After I finished talking with the Lord's negotiator, who was trying to get our properties for free, I called my wife and I told her what just happened. To my surprise, she said to me that I should give it to them so they would leave me alone. That night, I had another shock after I heard what she said to me. I was thinking that night and the next day, and I came to the conclusion that they put those words in her mouth or they made me hear what they wanted me to hear.

I've known my wife since 1975, and she wouldn't give away her home and her commercial property and go live with her daughter or live on the street. That was something very new. I thought to myself, What will be next? How far will they go? I had very bad experiences with them ever since November 12, 2012. First in my shop and then outside the shop. In November 2012, Sophia's mother told me that I couldn't sell my shop because that was her home.

It looks like they—those from there—needed places here to live. We sold our commercial property in summer of 2017. The new owners couldn't get permits yet for simple business. I believe those illegal occupants, who are calling it their home, had something to do with that.

No one can move them out of their home. Sophia's mother told me that's her home, that's their home.

October 30, 2014

My brother-in-law, Jerry Truskowski, is a doctor—gynecologist. He was living in Brooklyn, New York, but to keep his Polish doctor's license, he needed to go to Poland every few years and work there. While working in Polish hospitals in 2004, after checking up, they discovered cancer on his lung. They wanted to remove one of his lungs, but his second half wasn't 100 percent. He didn't have cancer there, but it wasn't too good. They removed a small piece.

Everything was good, but two years later, his cancer came back. They repeated the same way. Two years later there was something again. During the next operation, this time they removed the rest of that lung. When I spoke with him on the phone in spring of 2014, he told me that he had cancer all over and also in his heart and arteries. He told me he had about one year to live.

On February 1, 2015, I had been sitting in the third row
next to the Lord while praying where that white square with dot.

I had our Lord on the phone; I told him about my brother-in-law. The Lord asked me how he was, what kind of man he was, and I told the Lord that he is above average and he's a good man. I told the Lord that he is a gynecologist and that he was doing abortions. I said to the Lord that's his profession, but he did stop doing that.

He bought a painting, and he took that painting to famous, historical accounts of Jasna Gora Church and monastery, where its world-famous icon, the Black Madonna, was founded in 1382. Jasna Gora has been more than a spiritual home. Our Lady of Czestochowa in the chapel of our Lady. In their monastery is the famous painting of the Blessed Virgin. This painting of the Mother of God holding the Child Jesus in her arms bears the title: Our Lady of the Bright Hill. Pope Francis is going to Poland by the end of this month. He is going to be there for ten days. Chestochowa will be his primary stop.

On September 19, 2021, my wife was talking with her brother on phone. Her brother, Jerry Truskowskiy, who lives in the Warsaw, Poland. They had very long conversation; her brother said to her that he it is surprised and even shocked that he it's still alive; he said to my wife that he should have died long time ago. He has had cancer all over his body, around his heart and arteries. Just like he had in the 2014. Since then, nothing has changed; his health is on the same level. Seven years later he it is still alive and still working as the doctor at the age of seventy-four years old. He even said he doesn't believe his doctor, he said; he it's going to send the disk with his doctor's statements to his step-daughter who lives in the Boca Raton in Florida and works there in the hospital. He would like her to read the statement of that disk and pass to him what's on it. He doesn't believe what doctor keeps telling him. He a doctor himself, and he knows what's possible and what's impossible.

In October of 2014, when I had been talking with the Lord, I told him that my daughter was getting a divorce and her husband demands half of her money, which she made and saved before their marriage. She had in her saving account $270,000.

First parking. Lord parked his car here and walked across the street and waited for us till we got closer. He was standing where the 'X' is.

I said to the Lord, "She was working a few jobs as a dietitian. She had a job at Hakensack's Hospital, and she was working in a couple of other places. She was working hard to save that money." After I said that to the Lord, the Lord said he wouldn't get it, and he didn't get it. "Thank you, Lord." After I spoke with the Lord about her situation, her husband stopped demanding the money from her. He changed himself 180 degrees. But after the divorce, on some occasions, he said he wouldn't do that now. The Lord has power.

Nurse Linda, who was working at St. Clair's hospital in Sussex, NJ, is a living witness who assisted me when I had been bringing a man back to life who had died while we were standing by his bed. So, she is a living witness to the miracle that I performed.

Also, she called me from St. Clair's hospital on November 6, 2014, to let me know that my daughter was born, and that her mother, who is my guardian angel, asked me to choose a name for my daughter. With the nurse's help, I chose a name for her: Ramona. Now, Linda works in Sussex County. She continues to do good work and to help people.

One more thing, those medals that I received on the Roosevelt Aircraft carrier in June of 2016 from the president—my negotiator asked me what I wanted to do with those medals: keep them or send them to the museum. I told him, "Take them to the museum." I believe he took them to the Vatican museum. Or, instead, he could take them to Heaven's Kingdom Museum.

After I read the Wall Street Journal about Cardinals of Chicago and O'Malley of Boston going to have a meeting with Pope Francis in February, I wrote letters to Cardinals. I'm one hundred percent certain of that subject matter, because I received a message from the Lord telling me of that meeting. There is no room in the Roman Catholic Church for gays or child abusers. Also, those who cover up must be prosecuted. The Roman Catholic Church must be a good example, but it's not always like that. It's time for change.

One more thing in this letter: My first pilot was a helicopter pilot in the Polish army; that's why he got that job. He was also my guardian angel. When I had been visiting my brother up there, my guardian angel told me how he lost his life. He drove his car under the influence of alcohol, got into an accident, and killed himself and someone else. He is now working to become the best guardian angel he can be.

He asked me to remember him. He is about my age; I was born in 1947. It should be easy to find his records in the city of Legnica where he was a pilot, and I believe he was living there. I sent a letter to the archbishop of the archdiocese of Wroclaw, Poland.

On February 15, 2015, the Lord had been reading the Bible on the alter, by the pulpit on the left side where the yellow arrow indicates." AND "On February 8, 2015, I prayed with St. Pope John Paul II at the same church, with the Lord sitting a few rows in front of us. The Lord was sitting where that green arrow is pointing.

February 1, 2015

My guardian angel's father is a reporter at ABC News. His name is Jim D.

On February 1, 2015, at St. Francis de Sales Catholic Church in Vernon, I had been holding the Lord's hand while praying. Everyone saw the Lord at Church, but only I knew that was him. He was on film on the Church's camera. On February 8, 2015, I prayed with St. John Paul II at the same Church, with the Lord sitting a few rows in front of us. Everyone could see the Lord.

A few days later, the Lord told me that He was the one holding my hand while we prayed. He also told me his hands were as rough as forty-grade sandpaper, so that I would pay attention, and I did. He looked like he was eighty years old, but his hands felt like brick layers. He also told me that the man who was holding my hand while we prayed was St. John Paul II. After we finished the prayer, he squeezed my hand very hard. This was the first time the Lord had held my hand while I prayed. It was a transforming experience; I began to see and pray with the Lord more often.

Sometime before, my guardian angel did the same thing, holding my hand during prayer. Only three times in my life did somebody no closer than my wife hold my hand while praying. There was another time the Lord was reading. Everyone is registered and is appointed, but in this case, the Cardinal said they couldn't locate the man who was reading on the altar. I'm at Church almost every Sunday.

February 8, 2015
First Parking. Lord parked his car here. And walked across the street. And was waiting for us till we get closer. He was standing where the X is.

Once we got closer to him, he started walking to Church. The Lord did want me to follow him to the bench, where he was always sitting. The Lord did want me to sit next to him and pray with him. That wasn't a coincidence. The Lord had his plans. He walked to the sidewalk and had been waiting for me. Instead I did follow my wife, and she got me to the bench, where St. Pop John Paul II was sitting, and I prayed with him. I believe the highest power was involved in this. Instead, go and sit next to the Lord, some power pulled my wife to the bench where St. Pop John Paul II had been sitting. That wasn't a coincidence. Why didn't she go to a different bench? The Lord knew that St. Pop John Paul II is coming. He never before was waiting for me outside the Church. Some time later the Lord asked me why I didn't come that Sunday to sit next to him and pray with him. He said to me that he did want to pray with me. I did explain to him what happened. Looks like two powers are fighting for me.

On February 1, 2015, I had been sitting in the third row next to the Lord while praying. Where that yellow square with the black dot is. The Lord was always sitting there.

On February 8, 2015, I prayed with St. Pope John Paul II at the same church, with the Lord sitting a few rows in front of us. I prayed with St. Pope John Paul II where that yellow square with an X is.

On February 15, 2015, the Lord had been reading the Bible on the altar, by that pulpit on the left side.

February 15, 2015
On February 15, 2015, the Lord had been reading the Bible on an altar at the same Church, which is also on film and in the Cardinal's possession.

The Church also has that on camera; the Cardinal has copy. I believe it was about one week later after I prayed with St. John Paul II that the Lord was walking with me on the side of the Church. When we got close to Him, He was walking in front of us, and my wife was walking first; I was behind her. She chose a bench in the rear of the Church, and the Lord was always sitting in the second or third row. Sometime later, when I was talking to him, he asked me why I didn't come to sit next to him. He said he wanted to pray with me, but I told him that my wife was in front of me and she chose that bench in the back. The Lord and I continued talking, and he told me that he desired to sit with me in Church, so I would try to sit with him whenever I could.

Between January and March of 2015, I had been working on a new invention. I needed to research on the computer if something like that was already on the market. After some time I spent researching on the computer, to my big surprise, I found information about Mary Magdalene. Someone from France wrote that Mary Magdalene was a man. That really shocked me because for over two thousand years, we were hearing that Mary Magdalene was a woman. I thought to myself, One day I'm going to ask the Lord about this and I will straighten this out once and for all.

March 17, 2015
A few months later, on March 17, 2015, I had been talking with the Lord at my condominium for a few hours. I asked him if Mary Magdalene was a man, and his reply, to my shock was that she was a man. One day, this would be straightened out. I would also mention this to Cardinal at a later date on June 29, 2016, after the ceremony at St. Patrick's Cathedral, and then, once again I would be talking with Cardinal about this matter at the White House on Inauguration Day, on January 20, 2017, to which Cardinal said to me, "We suspect that."

on February 15, 2015 the Lord was reading the Bible on the alter but the pulpit on the left side

When I was talking with the Lord on March 17, 2015, I believe he was living at my condo for some time, because I had been talking with him many times, but not that long. I came home late and had a few glasses of wine, and after that I usually liked to talk. The Lord and I had very good conversation.

I don't remember how we started talking. I think the Lord asked me why I planted two chestnut seeds next to a tall cedar tree. I suppose that was an odd thing to do, so it makes sense that the Lord would question me. I told him I planted them all over, but these two just came up. He asked me why chestnuts were so important to me. I told Him I was born in the town of Kościan in Poland and by the river there, big chestnut trees were growing.

When I was a boy, in September when we had biology class, I would go with my teacher to the park to pick up chestnuts, acorns, and colored leaves. The Lord said he must go to see them himself; he could be there in no time. He then asked me why I was putting olive oil on my face, and I said the pharaohs used olive oil. He asked me how I knew that, and I told him I read a book about Egypt in Poland when I was in fifth grade. The book name was in Polish, FARAON, meaning PHARAOH.

The Lord would also ask me about things happening in the world. The Lord asked me what I do remember from that pharaoh book. Then I told him the story about someone who was killed, and there was someone killed, and police were investigating that crime, asking people if anyone saw someone in the area at that time. Someone said he saw a man walking by. They took him to court and made him guilty. When execution day came, the family was waiting outside when someone walked up to them and told them, "Be patient. Soon you will receive his body." The Lord asked me, "Do you think they did the right thing?"

I said, "No, they sentenced an innocent man. Did that do anything good, other than scare others?" The Lord seemed pleased with my answer. I never was sure if he was just making conversation or if he was testing my faith. I decided to ask him a few questions in return.

Also, the Lord asked me how we should sit at the table when we eat. I told him we should sit straight legs straight on the floor, feet together, only keep the left hand on the knee or just on the edge of the table. The Lord said that we should keep the fork close to the plate, not high like we would poke someone in the eye, and same with the knife. I said, "I'm good with the knife and fork."

I asked the Lord about the Great Flood—if that happened. He said, "God wouldn't do such a terrible thing." I told him that I believed him; I don't think it would be possible to fit all of the species on a boat. We continued talking about religion, and I told him used to have crosses in our school classrooms. He was surprised because, at that time, Poland was a communist country. The Lord was proud of Polish people, because Polish people are very good Catholics. We talked about everything. The Lord also told me that being gay is a sin.

On January 13, 2016, a limousine picked up me from the front entrance

The Lord was only once reading the Bible at Church altar on 2-15-15. The Cardinal said they couldn't locate that man. Whoever was reading and is knowing and has appointments for that hour and that day. That man was the Lord. He has no address. He was living at my home and is still, on and off.

About a year later, on the night of January 6, 2016, I was baptized in a pond on the golf course in front of my condominium. The Lord and my guardian angel told me about the baptism. I don't remember getting baptized. It happened at night, and I was hypnotized. When I woke up in the morning, I was missing my pajama pants. I looked all over for them. Finally, I found them in the laundry basket all wet. Later, I was told by my guardian angel and the Lord that I was baptized. I was supposed to have been taken from the earth a long time ago, but it looked like my job was not done here yet.

When I was a boy, in September, when we had biology class, I would go with my teacher to the park to pick up chestnuts, acorns, and colored leaves. The Lord said he must go to see them himself; he could be there in no time. He then asked me why I was putting olive oil on my face, and I said the pharaohs used olive oil. He asked me how I knew that, and I told him I read a book

I had also been talking with the Lord about Popes; after I prayed with the Lord and St. Pope John Paul II at St. Francis De Sales Church in Vernon, NJ, I praised St. Pope John Paul II for his hard work and his achievements for the Roman Catholic Church and other religions. I said to the Lord that I really liked St. Pope John Paul II.

On February 13, 2016 I had lunch at this restaurant which is located at the bottom of ski slope in New Jersey I met those 2 man in black suites in this restaurant on January 13, 2016

The Lord replied, "We saved his life after he was shot six times by a Turkish citizen."

Then the Lord asked me what I thought about Pope Benedict XVI. I said he was just like his former boss. They both were good Roman Catholic Church leaders. Then the Lord asked me what I thought about Pope Francis.

I replied, "I don't know him that well yet."

At the end of my conversation with the Lord on March 17, 2015, I said to the Lord, "It's good to have someone around to talk with. It's very easy to communicate with the Lord. He is a good speaker, mentor, and teacher. He always has been."

The Lord replied, "Just said so."

January 13, 2016

I like to watch the History and Discovery channels. Many times, I saw two men in black suits; white shirts; black ties; black, tall hats; and black sunglasses. Those two guys always looked like perfect twins, just like they were made from wax, tall, perfect build.

It was a beautiful, sunny day. I thought to myself, What I will do today? After some thought, I decided to go for lunch at Great Gorge Resort. I loved walking, so even though it was a half-mile away, I walked the whole way there. I sat outside with my face toward the slope and the sun. I ordered a nice, hot sandwich and a beer, and after I finished, I went back inside. The atmosphere was great with its nice loud music.

The restaurant inside was full. After a couple of hours, two guys in black suits and sunglasses came up to me and said, "The limousine outside is waiting for you." I went downstairs and there was a black stretch limousine with the door wide open and a beautiful blond girl standing beside it, welcoming me inside. That girl was my former next-door neighbor. She and her family moved out in 2014, and she went on to college at Syracuse University in NY. Her mother was transferred to Atlanta, GA. She was on winter break and was working at the resort. The management of the resort sent the limousine because they had an interest in building the statues we had previously discussed, bringing tourists to the town and growing business. Jesus Christ on the ski slopes—in Vernon, NJ—more people would come here than to the Vatican or Bethlehem. As you can see, they had planned it all well; they sent a limo because they did not want me to party there. Also, they sent that blond girl so I would trust them that they were taking me home or right to the place. They had so much power over me I did not ask them where I was going.

It was an important day. It was January 13, 2016. It is a long story, but I will make short for now. My pilot and a few invisible people flew in my helicopter to a Sussex hospital in NJ. I'm 99.9 percent certain the Lord had been on that helicopter as well.

Sometime after New Year's Day of 2016, I was talking with the general manager of Minerals Resort and Spa about meeting the Lord on a ski slope and how I have been talking to him since then. This was the general manager of the property where I first met the Lord. The resort owns the whole mountain and many other resorts in Vernon, NJ. I had plans to build a statue of the Lord Jesus Christ in a place, so I met him there. I did want to build directly on their land.

I told the manager that I saw the Lord many times in different spots in Vernon, NJ. I also told him a story about a woman I met at a Montclair, NJ, hospital to prove to him my power and miracles.

I told him that when I was walking in one of the hallways, I saw and heard a woman yelling, "Jesus! Jesus, take me!" over and over. The door was open, so I stood in front her room and blessed her. A few minutes later, she was smiling, and two hours later, she was dressed and ready to leave. I asked her what was wrong with her, but she said the doctor didn't know. She had a big smile on her face. I heard two nurses passing me saying that we were lucky we were blessed.

I told him that I had to go to see Nurse Linda at St. Clair Hospital in Sussex, NJ. I later wrote to her, and she called me from the hospital after my daughter was born, and my daughter's mother is my guardian angel. That's 100 percent proof. She died when she was fourteen years old and came to guard me when she was nineteen years old. She got the job because she speaks Polish and English.

After I told this story to the manager, he told me we needed more to move forward with this project of building statues in places where miracles happened. A lot of tourists would come, and the resort could build hotels and more.

A couple of hours later, I got a call from the manager. We talked about miracles, Nurse Linda from St. Clair Hospital, and my daughter, whose mother is my guardian angel. The manager said, "We will come to pick you up and we will drive you to your helicopter, and you will fly to St. Clair Hospital.

Claire Hospital in Sussex to talk with Nurse Linda about the previous miracle experiences she witnessed." They wanted me to stop partying, go to the hospital, and ask Nurse Linda to write them a letter and explain what happened in the past. They needed proof of my miracles.

I called the hospital and I asked for Nurse Linda. She was there, so I asked her if they had a helicopter landing pad, and she said they do. She asked me,

"Are you going to fly that black one?" I told her, "No, I have new one—red." They asked me to fly by helicopter because it looked better. It was a coincidence that a higher authority was involved in this whole thing that day.

On January 13, 2016 I did enter this door on my way to meet the Nurse Linda Kelly.

On January 17. 2016, at this building I had dinner, press conference, and cocktail with the Lord.

After I started talking to Nurse Linda about my daughter, Ramona, who was born in the hospital, I asked her if she could write me a letter with all of the stories, and she said she could. I don't know how we got to the point when I told her about that woman at Montclair Hospital. When she heard that, she asked me if I could help a dying patient there, whom I then brought back to life.

When we got inside the patient's room, he was still alive. After a couple of minutes, he died. The monitor showed that he was dead. I said to him in Polish, "Wróć bracie do zdrowia, bądź zdrowy znowu." "Come back to health; be healthy again." Then the man opened his eyes and looked at me. I said to him, "Relax and you will be okay." The doctor and nurse were shocked. I left the room with Nurse Linda and the doctor. They hugged me, and Nurse Linda was kissing me until the doctor told her to stop.

Then Linda and I stepped out and I showed her my new red helicopter. I promised her that one day we would fly to New York City for lunch. We haven't flown yet, but one day we may. Linda is very important to me; it is important that, someday, we fly in my helicopter to New York City. I want to do that for her.

35

I went to the hospital to get something from the past, and I also performed a miracle. That's what the owners of the resort wanted to see. When miracles happened on the ski slope, that means tourists will come. When lots of tourists come, they will need a place to stay, eat, and there will be more attractions. They are interested in building big businesses; they're just lucky.

In a couple of days, I was scheduled to have a press conference about my miracles. After the King, the press conference started there. The higher power coordinated the whole day and also other events. That was on 1-17-2016. I had been moving from place to place until the time was right for the press conference. I left my home in the morning and I went for lunch with my organizer. When I was done meeting with him, the press conference was ready and waiting for me. Someone was directing me. It was someone I didn't recognize, or even know. It was as though someone else was guiding my footsteps. I didn't know anything about it; a higher power got me there on time.

On January 17. 2016, I ate my breakfast by this bar in Vernon, New Jersey. The Lord had been standing or sitting next to me because couple days later he told me that I could eat that omelet with fork only. Then he adds that I'm good with fork and knife.

There was a small incident during the press conference, though I didn't organize any of it. An eighteen-year-old girl ran toward me, dropped on her knees, slid like she was on ice, wrapped her arms around my legs, looked up, and asked me, "Would you marry me?"

I asked her, "How old are you, child?"

Her answer was, "I'm eighteen. I don't need permission."

I lifted her up and I said, "I'm sixty-nine years old."

She said, "You don't look sixty-nine; you look like you are in your forties." She turned her head toward reporters and said, "Right?" They said, "Right." She asked, "Why do you look younger? Because you came from there? From above?" I said to the young girl, "One day you will find your prince." They were reporters from ABC and NBC, including SK. Also there were reporters from other stations.

On January 17, 2016, at the Red Trail Lodge, Vernon, NJ, 07462, the time was right! Those young men I believe were angels delivered me to Red Trail Lodge, and they disappeared.

January 17, 2016

I got out of bed at seven o'clock in the morning. I had a couple cups of coffee, then I took a shower. After I dressed myself, I decided to go for walk on the golf course. I was walking for about one hour when I decided to go for breakfast at Kites Restaurant at Minerals Resort, where I was living at the time. I had a huge omelette, orange juice, and, of course, coffee. They treated me well there, especially after the miracle I performed at St. Clair Hospital in Sussex, NJ, a few days prior. I think it was the combination of the miracle I preformed and the possibility of expanding the resort made them very sweet to me.

After breakfast, I went for another walk for about two hours on the golf course. After my walk, I went to Great Gorge Ski Resort to watch a football game between the Panthers vs. Seahawks. I had good company: a bunch of young people were sitting next to me and we had good conversations, especially after a couple of drinks. After a good couple of hours, we decided to go to Red Tail Lodge Ski Resort, which is located on the same Route 94, about one mile north from Great Gorge Ski Resort. Once we got there, somehow, we split up.

However, I decided to make the most of my time at Red Tail Lodge. There were a few nice restaurants. I chose the very elegant one. It was big, with a cathedral ceiling, huge stone fireplace, leather armchairs and couches, a very nice bar, paintings, good service, and very good food. I decided to have a meal there and watch some football on the television. Since I was by myself, I sat by the beautiful bar and ordered a glass of white wine. After a few sips, a young man came up and sat next to me. He was around forty years old. I don't remember how we started talking, but we were talking about building monuments in places where I have been talking to the Lord. We planned to build hotels and more.

For the first time, I found out that he was my organizer and negotiator, sent by the Lord. He eventually organized trips by helicopter to NYC and limos from Pier 59 to the Plaza Hotel; he dressed me in a white suit and my guardian angel in a white skirt suit and drove us to St. Patrick Cathedral and to Roosevelt Aircraft Carrier—all of those things he organized without my knowledge. He was sent here from above, from Lord Jesus Christ.

His job is like the secretary of state's job. We have negotiated deals with future partners together. We made deals 50-50. He is the leader of a powerful country. After that, we shook our

Supper. Spa, 3 pools and Gym.

January 17, 2017, in this huge lodge it is few nice restaurants. I had dinner at Hawk's N.... Press conference I had on second floor, cocktails with the Lord I had on third floor, at Schu... restaurant.

I had a press conference there. The Sports bar is above upstairs.

After press conference on January 17, 2016, I had cocktail with the Lord; we were sitting by the bar, where that yellow square it is. Also, I met with mother of that young man, whom I brought back to life.

We shook our hands, and the deal was done. He got up and he left. After I paid for my food and wine, I also left. My negotiator was sent to work with me from above. I had a feeling that he would do a great job, especially since he was sent directly from the Lord. I knew that I couldn't handle all of the details of travel, business arrangements, and work myself, so I was grateful that the Lord sent me someone to help.

After I brought the man back to life, someone organized a press conference at Red Tail Lodge in Vernon, NJ. It makes sense; of course, there were people who wanted to know about my miracle. There were reporters from ABC, from MSNBC, and reporters from other stations.

I had been sitting in the chair where that Yellow sticker is on January 17, 2016 with the Lord sitting on left side next to me.

When I entered the huge conference room for the press conference, someone had loudly yelled, "Stop the music! Here comes the King! He is the new King." That someone was the Lord; he told me himself a couple of days later. That man asked me what He is going to do since I'm the new King. I told him He is going to be retired.

From NBC reporter Steve K. and reporter from ABC, Martha R. She asked me the most questions. The woman asked me the most questions and asked me about the helicopter. There were other reporters with questions. After I finished paying for my meal, I stepped out and entered a huge ballroom-like place with live music.

I was shocked. I said, "What is this?" I didn't know what was going on. At that moment, lights were going on and camera lights were blinking. I still didn't know what this was all about. They asked me the first question.

"Sir, you have been separated in 1995."

I replied, "Mind your own business and keep your nose clean." He got me very upset because there were so many interesting things that happened in the last few days and he asked me that nonsense question.

Next, he asked me, "Sir, why did you have that [Sikorsky] powerful, fast Sikorsky helicopter? What did you need that for?" By now I knew he was not my friend. Instead of asking me questions, he was attacking me.

I replied to him, "You go to him and tell him that I have a too fast and too powerful helicopter. If I had a slower helicopter, that would be too late for him."

Then the reporter from ABC asked me what I did when I got to the hospital. I told her once I got inside the hospital, I met with Nurse Linda Kelly. She was waiting for me because I needed her letter about previous experiences she witnessed. After I told her the story about the woman at Montclair Hospital, she told me that they had a dying young man and asked if I could help him. I met Nurse Linda before, and I liked her very much and would do a lot for her. I said without hesitation, "Let's do it." After I said that to her, she took the microphone and started yelling, "Doctor [his name which I don't remember]! Please come to the front desk for an emergency assistant." She was very emotional by now, and she was repeating each time louder and louder; time was running out, and she was very nervous.

Restaurant and Pub

By this bar.

At this ski lodge I had lunch on January 17, 2016. I had been sitting in that chair where that yellow arrow indicates.

When the doctor came, she told him that I was going to try to heal that dying young man. I was kind of surprised that the man came from the street, and the doctor and nurse took him to the emergency room to see the dying patient, trusting me and fully believing me that I was going to make a miracle for their patient by healing him and spreading good news about their hospital.

Once we got inside that patient's room, he was still alive, but one minute later, he died. I looked at him and I said in Polish, "Bracie, wróć do zdrowia, bądź znów zdrowy." He opened his eyes and looked at me. I still remember his blue eyes; he was in pain and scared. The doctors and nurses were shocked; they couldn't believe their own eyes, a miracle in their hospital. They saw that monitor on the wall showing he died. The monitor was making that sound, "bee, bee, pee, pee," which means that the heart stopped beating.

After that first shock, the nurse asked me, "What did you say to him?"

I said in English, "Brother, come back to health, be healthy again."

45

The reporter from ABC asked me, "Is he your brother?"

I said, "No, we are all brothers and sisters."

Then she asked me what that meant in English, what I said to that patient in Polish. Stive K said that very quickly in perfect Polish. Next, she asked me if they saw my books in which I have recorded my patents.

I replied, "No, because many of them are still pending." Next, he was describing how I was dressed, I believe for NBC records. White leather sneakers, a little dirty. I said I have been walking on the golf course and also I went to the ski slope where I met the Lord.

Then he asked me whose designer jeans I was wearing. I answered Armani, and then he said, "He's wearing navy-blue suede leather bomber-style jacket." Next, he said I was wearing a sweatshirt and cashmere scarf. He told me that sweatshirts were out of style.

I replied, "Sweatshirts are back big time." He asked me what brand, and I said, "All." I asked him when the last time he went shopping was. His answer was that he's been buying online.

Then the reporter from ABC asked what designer clothes I've been buying. I said, "Armani, Canali, Givenchy, Christian Dior, Michael Kors."

"What shoes?"

"Aldo."

"How much did you pay?"

"A hundred and twenty dollars."

She was shocked and repeated, "A hundred and twenty dollars for shoes?" Then she asked what kind of jewelry I own. I said that I'm not into jewelry and watches. I told her I had a nice gold Omega watch and I gave it to my grandson when he was two years old.

She asked, "A gold watch to a two-year-old child?" I bought that watch at the New York City Macy's in 1974 and I paid seven hundred dollars for it. Back then that was a lot of money.

Then she started asking me about our judicial system. I replied, "It's far from perfect. It sometimes feels like it's still in the pharaohs' era with a lot of people who are innocent in prison, and after they're released, we don't want to pay them for those years they spent in prison."

"How about Israel and the land have been occupying since the 1967 war?"

"They must return to Palestinian people."

"What do you think about the Jewish people?"

"Jewish people are very nice, hardworking people who suffered a lot since the Romans and are still suffering wherever they live."

"What do you think about the Iraq War?"

"Sooner rather than later he's going to stand in front of a judge and he will be asked tough questions. When you're the big kid in the classroom, you have no right to be stealing lunch money from smaller kids. Or if you're the president from a powerful country, you don't have the right to go and destroy some other country."

The reporters asked me many more questions about religion. Once again, they asked me about Christmas. I told him Christmas was, is, and will be forever. He asked, "How about other religions?"

I said, "You have what you choose. Be happy and celebrate the way you should." After that, I never heard anyone complaining about Christmas's name.

He also asked where I had lived, and I said on the other side of the valley, about three miles, because he wanted to go and see. I told them to go on that side because the view from there of the ski slopes with lights on is beyond imagination. He also took the directions to my auto-body dealership in Sussex,

NJ. He called me in the summer of 2016 and told me he loved that car in the showroom, a 1934 Ford two-door coupe. At that time, that car wasn't completed, it was apart. Steve told me that he would like to drive this car. He wasn't the only one. Also, he went to see the house. It was an almost ten-thousand-square-feet Mediterranean-style house without an obstructed view.

Minerals Resort and Spa. Upstairs its a Restaurant-Bar. Where I met the Lord on February 19, 2016.

I was also asked about shootings in schools, Churches, malls, and everywhere. I said, "Why has no one done any research yet on who's raising those kids? Is it single parents, or are father and mother working and kids are unsupervised?"

Later, after that press conference, I heard on the news Diane S. was doing research, talking to President BO on the Roosevelt Aircraft Carrier, on the end of June 2016, about this subject, and he told me Diana S was working on that, and she will published a book about her discovery. I was happy.

A reporter from ABC asked me if I was going to heal other people. I said to her, "Maybe here and there." She asked me how I was going to choose when to do so, and I said, "I will be in some place and something happened." She said, "There are so many diseases. People are dying." I told her that we are born to die.

The reporter from ABC asked me why I have such a nice face color. I told her I'm using oil from orange peels. I said, "So many women are asking me that. I thought they wanted to pick me up." She asked me, "Of what age?" I said, "From eighteen to eighty years old." Really, I think the color in my face comes both from the orange peels and from spending time with the Lord outside.

Then the reporters asked me if I cooked. "Yes," and I gave them recipes. "Do you do laundry and iron?" "Yes, and shirt sleeves without creases. To avoid creases, simply don't do over the edge; stop at an eighth of an inch before the sleeve's edge." There were so many questions about my daily life, like cooking and laundry. I suppose they wanted to know about how someone who can perform miracles lives their daily life.

With all of these questions, it was a long press conference. The reporter from ABC asked me if that was my first press conference, and I said, "Yes." She told me that I'm good. She asked me if I would do an interview with Barbara Walters for two million dollars.

I said, "I would have to prepare myself."

She said, "Don't worry about her; you are better." This was when things really started to pick up; before all of this, I had only spoken with the guardian angels and the Lord in private. But now all of my knowledge and wisdom was starting to become public. This was a turning point in my life.

Lord's car parked under apple tree.

On February 19, 2016, the Lord and I were sitting in front of the fireplace. I was sitting in left side in armchair and the Lord on right side.

I liked that press conference. I didn't want it to stop. At the end they thanked me for the interview. After the press conference the band started playing again and a young woman in her early twenties came up to me and asked me if I would like to dance. I said yes and we danced, and once we finished, we got a standing ovation. That young woman was my guardian angel, Mother of Ramona, at that time, and now also Gabriela.

After that dance I went upstairs. First the manager came up to me and congratulated me, said that was a good press conference and that it came out good. After I split with the resort manager, the mother of that young man who I brought back to life came up to me. She said, "Sir, I heard that you were here, and I came here to say thank you for bringing my son back to life." She introduced herself. I met her in 2004 in Sussex, NJ, at the Sussex Inn. She was a teacher, and her friends were also teachers. They were living across the street on Van Blarcorn Ct. Sussex, NJ, 07461. I had been living on 8 Blarcorn Ct. Sussex, NJ. That's why she knew me very well, seeing me by my house while visiting her friends. She said, "Sir, you flew your personal helicopter to the hospital and you gave him another, a second life." She asked if she could give me a hug.

I said, "Yes, you can."

After she left, I thought to myself, I need to sit down by the bar and relax. After I sat down, two minutes later an older man came up and asked if he could sit next to me. I don't know why, but I ordered one Rcmy Martin French Cognac for him. "I believe he made me, or I had a feeling that's the Lord." And I also ordered one for me. One shot was sixteen dollars. We were talking about different things. Next round, my new friend ordered.

He said to the young woman behind the bar, "I would like the same for nine dollars."

She agreed with this price and the woman behind the bar said, "Nine dollars."

Restaurant with fireplace in Vernon where I met the Lord on February 19, 2016. The Lord and I were sitting in front of the fireplace. I was sitting on left side in armchair and the Lord on right side.

Then he quickly changed the price and said to her, "Eight dollars." She agreed with him again and said, "Eight dollars." And that's how much he paid.

He paid eight dollars for each, which is normally sixteen dollars for one. After she accepted his price of eight dollars, he turned his head towards me and said to me, "See? The Lord can do anything." He wanted to show me who he was. These are all true stories. After we finished, he asked me if I wanted him to drive me home, but I wasn't ready yet.

I said, "No thank you, I will walk home."

After he left, I went downstairs and I met the mayor and police chief. After the mayor realized what I did on January 13, 2016, he got excited and offered to drive me home by himself, but both him and the police chief drove me home. We started talking about how I was going to change this town. I said, "We will build an airport by the railroad for small jets." They were very excited. When you have the Lord behind your back, you can get it done, not only paying half the price for a drink at the bar.

Before the press conference, I had a very important business negotiation with a world leader; I will keep his name a secret for now. My negotiator had been living in Russia before he died. He was an extremely intelligent man. The Lord was the architect of that negotiation; it was all planned. My negotiator was the executor; you can't beat a team like that.

A couple of days later, I found out that it was the Lord who yelled "Stop the music! Here comes the King! He is the new King." Like, you see, the whole thing was planned from above.

After that press conference, I was on the front page of every newspaper. The Lord was next to me all day. He was even beside me at Kites when I had breakfast a few days later, and He told me that I could eat my omelet with just a fork. I told him I could, but it was a cheese, ham, and vegetable omelet. He said "Yes," and also said I'm good with a knife and fork.

February 2016
They have reasons, because if I would move out of New Jersey, they would have to go back. But they don't want to go back. They told me, "You don't know how they are there or where they came from."

The Lord's car.

The Lord also told me, "You don't know how they are there."

April 13, 2016

At night on April 13, 2016, my angels took me up there above to show me how people were living there who committed terrible crimes here on earth.

I had been there where they came from. That's not a vacation place, but you only get what you deserve.

I've written letters to the Cardinal, Barbara from ABC, and Steve K. from NBC. That was in 2016. wanted to write my true story in the book, but she told me that someone came to her and told her they would destroy her if she wrote it. They also told the Cardinal to not do what I had asked him to do. I believe he did the same with the others. He told the Cardinal he would send back those two guardian angels; after that would be the end of the world.

You don't have to be afraid of him; just throw him out. I'm writing so much about this because here is more proof of what is going on. It should be easy to find a deed or get a copy of it to my condo.

February 19, 2016

The weather was very nice, like a usual afternoon. I went for a long walk on the golf course. I was walking for about two hours. When I finished walking, something or someone told me, directed me to go to Kite's Restaurant-Bar at Minerals Resort for coffee. I never went just for coffee, but that day a higher power, just like a magnet, was pulling me there. When I got inside, I went straight to the fireplace. I sat down in a nice leather armchair in front of the big fireplace. I ordered a cup of coffee.

After sitting and drinking hot coffee for about twenty minutes, along came a man, and he asked me if anybody was sitting there. I said nobody, and he took a menu and ordered something to eat, along with two Bloody Mary drinks. After he finished eating and we finished our drinks, he said, "I want to show you a nice place in Hamburg by Route 94 about four miles away." The Lord has powers and you can't say no; everything was organized.

A few weeks later, the Lord organized a dinner with my mother, father, grandmother, brother, sister Helen, and sister Praksida. They died a long time ago, but there are recordings of them on a restaurant camera, which is also in Cardinal D's possession. That dinner was held at Craven Thai in Hamburg, NJ.

I said, "Good. Let's go." He drove us there in his Toyota Prius hybrid. His car is still parked under the apple tree near where I am living.

We went there and sat down, and we ordered a light dinner with two drinks. A few tables away by the window, there was a group of people standing by the table and looking at us. A man who was with them took a couple of steps toward us and stopped. Then the Lord Jesus Christ said to me, "That's your family. Go talk to them. Talk to them in Polish because they can't speak English." I was shocked. I said, "What should I say?"

Cravin Thai Restaurant in Hamburg

On February 19. 2016, I had dinner by this table with my family who's died long time ago. At that time this table was set for 6.

The Lord parked his car at the Minerals Resort parking lot in summer of 2017. It was park there till summer of 2018. I took picture of that Toyota Prius on June 20, 2018. Whatever the Lord does, he does for a reason. I've known the Lord for a long time. Why did the Lord park his car under the apple tree? After I wrote a letter to the Cardinal, Pope, Pope XVI, and most Cardinals, archbishops, Bishop J. from the diocese, the head of our Church in Vernon, New Jersey, the Lord's car was removed and placed somewhere.

Lord's car under apple tree.

On February 19, Lord drove us here in his Toyota Prius Hybrid.

Me and the Lord were sitting by this table.

The Lord's Toyota Prius hybrid was parked under this apple tree.

Me and Lord were standing on right side of that tree, that was on March 25,
2016. We were standing where that white dot is.

Four Augusta Drive Vernon, New Jersey.

This building is located on 4 Augusta Drive and first golf's fairway. On March 25, 2016, I saw Lord was walking on its all dressed in black. The Lord's Toyota Prius was parked in front of this building in Building 4, Augusta Drive, Unit 7, and had been living there. A female angel, she was living there for few years. She did that nice landscaping around that end of the building between 2015 and 2019; many times she walked around the pond. Barefoot, she was wearing white dress. Even on chilly early mornings. She was washing her bare feet in the pond. I had been talking with her many times by the pond, also when she was working in her garden, by her condominium. She had always a lot of beautiful flowers growing in her garden by her condominium. She bought and did plant many nice trees and bushes there too. She was using water from brook which was running through her garden. I believe she moved out in summer of 2019. Before she moved out she did ask her neighbors to take care of her garden. Its very sad because her former garden, it is partially overgrown. She was driving white Mercedes model GLS-250.

Side of the building Dr. U

He said, "People on that side of the firmament are not allowed to shake hands or kiss each other, but you can give them a hug and give them a kiss on their cheeks." So, I got up and walked toward them. I think I first hugged my grandma; she said, "I remember you coming with your father to visit us. You were so blond." I said, "And I'm still blond, Grandma. My hair is platinum blond."

For the first time, I saw my oldest sister, Praxida. She was born in 1932 and died of an infection in 1937. She was five years old. When I met them, she was a five-year-old girl standing there. They all passed away: my grandma in early 1950, my mother in 1960, my father in 1993, my sister Helen in 2004, and my brother Jurek in 2005. Thank you, Lord Jesus Christ, for bringing them there and giving me the opportunity to have dinner with them, and, of course, with You.

She was washing her bare feet in this pond.

I wrote a letter to the Cardinal, Pope, Pope Francis, and most Cardinals, archbishops, the bishop from the diocese, the head of our Church in Vernon, and Father. I wrote to them about the Lord's car and the whole story. I asked them to check the history of that car and if it would be possible to take it to a car museum. It was removed from there.

There was another time that I transported mysteriously; one morning, I woke up in Vatican City in 2016 with my guardian angel and negotiator. I woke up walking on St. Peter's Square toward St. Peter's Basilica. On my left side was my guardian angel, and on my right side was my negotiator, who was carrying an important letter to Pope Francis. Pope Francis had been waiting for me at his office. The negotiator must have told him that I was coming.

I had a nice conversation with him, sharing the experiences I had in Argentina in 1975. How I got back to New Jersey—the same way I got to Vatican City.

After my meeting with Pope Francis, I went back to New Jersey for some time. In front of my window, about forty to fifty feet up, there was a pond in 2015. 2016 was a drought; there was no rain for a long time. The pond was almost empty. I had been worried about the fish, frogs, turtles, and all the things living there. There was no rain, but the pond was rising until it was full.

When I had been talking with the manager of the resort in 2016, I told him we filled up that pond in 2015 and in 2016 too. In the winter of 2015 into 2016, that was the start of the drought. He asked me if I could make snow for them on the ski slopes. I did so, which brought many people to the ski resort. There was another press conference about the miracle I had performed.

After that conference, I wrote only about things I could prove. Tons of other things happened, but who would believe them? You may not believe some things, but all of those records are there.

March 25, 2016

I had been walking on Port Royal from Minerals Spa at Great Gorge in Vernon, NJ, toward my home. After I walked about a quarter of a mile, I noticed a man walking on the golf course limping. He was dressed completely in black; he was wearing black sunglasses, even on a cloudy day, and in his right hand he was holding a long stick, but this time the stick was black. I thought to myself, That's the Lord. He was walking on the grass. I turned on the golf cart path. I had been speed-walking very fast towards him. The Lord knew that I was chasing him, and finally I caught up with him.

I said hello, and he said hello back. We shook our hands and introduced ourselves. I don't remember the name he said. I asked him where he lived, and he told me he lived in Vernon. We walked to the pond, we stopped under the cedar tree with the view of my condo on the other side, and I showed him where I lived. I told him I had been living there since February 2005 and explained that my wife and I really liked living there. I pointed to the stone wall by the evergreens and beautiful cedar trees. I said that I loved nature. He told me that I was like his friend who also loved nature.

I knew that was him even though he looked different this time. However, I reacted as if I just met my old friend. We just acted like we didn't know each other. I knew that was Jesus Christ, but somehow, I couldn't say that day, "Lord, how are you?" because he looked different. I was not 100 percent sure.

After a few minutes, we split up. I don't know why I didn't invite him to my home for a cup of coffee. Maybe he made it that way, as if they are not allowed to eat or drink in someone's house.

Spring 2016
In the spring of 2016, I started to worry about my relationship with the Lord. I asked the Lord if he liked me. He said, "No." I asked why, and his answer was, "Because you have too much power." The Lord told me I had power over him; he has different powers. I can send all of them back except those two guardian angels.

Sophia's mother was my guardian angel. She was that blond lady who pushed me off of that wall because she was jealous. That's why they removed her from here. Sophia's mother—once they took her back, but after a few months—came back. They knew where they would go. They asked me to have mercy on them.

April 2016
In April of 2016, at Chase Bank in Ramsey, NJ, the Lord was standing next to me, and I was talking to him. He then went away from me. But a few days later, we picked up our conversation. We met up at Minerals Golf. The Lord was dressed in total black, and in his right hand, he was holding a black, shepherd-like walking stick. I was walking next to him and talking with him. He informed me that I would be needed on earth; I would be needed to complete many more miracles and good deeds on earth. I would be very influential and would meet with many politicians and world leaders.

April 13, 2016
Golf Course

Golf Course 1st Fairway

On March 25, 2016, walking from spa I noticed man walking - limping on golf's first fairway, dressed complete in black, even on that cloudy day he was wearing black sunglasses, also that time his walking stick was black. Once I noticed him right away, I knew that's the Lord, I made quick plan, to walk fast on golf path to catch up with him. He is the Lord, he knew my plan, so he slow down. I caught up with him where that X it's.

On June 29 this helicopter landed by the pond.

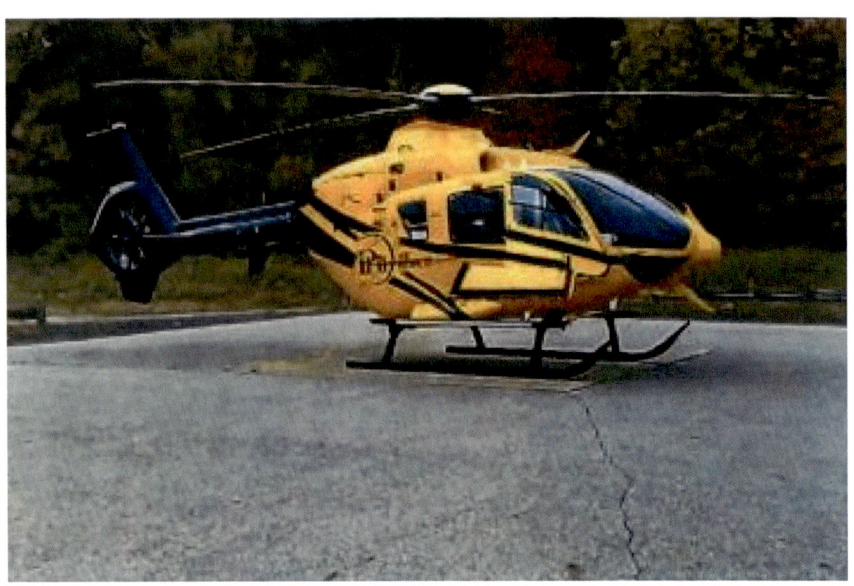

My helicopter's landing pad in Vernon.

Plaza Hotel in New York City

My helicopter's landing pad in New York City.

Me and Little Angel were drove by the Secret Service to this plaza hotel
then we were dressed in white.

Plaza Hotel

Before the Lord's car was moved to the parking of Mineral's Resort and Spa and parked under the apple tree, it was parked in front of building number four, Augusta Drive, Vernon, NJ, 07462. I believe Lord was living in that building or building number six. In January of 2017, I saw the Lord and two other men standing next to his car; also, there was a towing truck at that location. The Lord's car was parked there till summer of 2017. The Lord's car wasn't used. The window was little bit open, and a sticker was placed on the side window. A warning sticker. When I was talking with the Lord and the little angel in my kitchen with the Lord toward the end of May 2017, I did ask him what was wrong with his car; he replied that it was broken, and they towed it to the mechanic.

Roosevelt Aircraft Carrier

On the end of June 2016 these two F-16 did escort my to " Roosevelt Aircraft Carrier."

This building its located on 4 Augusta Drive and first golf's fairway. On March 25, 2016, I saw Lord was walking on it all dressed in black. The Lord's Toyota Prius was parked in front of this building in Building 4, Augusta Drive, Unit 7, and had been living there. A female angel, she was living there for few years. She did that nice landscaping around that end of the building between 2015 and 2019; many times she walked around the pond. Barefoot, she was wearing white dress. Even on chilly early mornings. She was washing her bare feet in the pond. I talked with her many times by the pond, also when she was working in her garden. By her condominium she always had a lot of beautiful flowers growing in her garden by her condominium. She bought and did plant many nice trees and bushes there too. She was using through her garden. I believe she moved out in summer of 2019. Before she moved out., she did ask her neighbors to take care of her garden. It's very sad because her former garden was overgrown.

St. Patrick's Cathedral in New York City. Me and little angel were married
here by Cardinal on June 29, 2016

At night on April 13, 2016, my angels took me up above to show me how people were living there who committed terrible crimes here on earth. I was talking to my former employee who had worked for me for two and a half years as an auto-body man. I believe in 1984 he started his own business. He ran his business till he died of cancer. Before he died, when I talked to him I noticed his voice was rough. Then a few weeks later I was talking again to him and his voice was still rough.

I said to him, "You better go to the doctor for a checkup." He went to the doctor in Brooklyn, New York. Once he opened the door, the doctor told him he had cancer. He asked the doctor how he knew, and he went for a second opinion to a doctor in Jersey City, New Jersey. The doctor asked him if he was smoking, he said yes, and she told him that he could smoke, that it wouldn't make any difference. We were good friends, and he died a few months later. The day he died, he came to my garage and was knocking with pipe on the wall. A couple hours later his partner called me and said that Andrzej Poklika-jew died. He was at my garage for about one week. He knew I was coming there, so he was waiting for me.

When he was walking toward me, he was smiling and saying, "You, you, you, he meant you will be judging."

I asked, "How did you get to that? What have you done?" He said he drove a car under the influence of alcohol, hit someone, killed him, and took off. He asked me not to send him to Hell. I said, "Do you think you will go to Heaven?" He said, "No, but not there," and once again he asked me to re-member him.

"Don't forget me," he said.

Dear reader, no one wants to go to Hell; it's worth it to be a good person. Heaven, Purgatory, and Hell are real. He was a great man. He would help you if you needed his help. I asked my former employee if he was knocking with pipe on the wall. His reply was that he had been walking along the wall and at the same time was hitting with pipe on the wall. After he spent one week at my garage, he decided to go above. He wasn't in a rush because he knew what he had done, and he knew, somehow, what was waiting for him and where he was going.

I got married at this cathedral
with Little Angel on June 29, 2016

I'm living at a Four Seasons resort. A lot of bad things happened over here, like at any resort, casino, racetrack; there are plenty of bad people around. I met many people there, even two policemen and state troopers who were there. Some of them asked me to have mercy on them. I met molesters, people who committed murders, rapists, and people who committed other terrible crimes.

On the end of the tour, Lord Jesus Christ came up to me. He was dressed in black uniform, black shirt, and black pants. When I saw him there, I was kind of shocked. I asked him, "What are you doing here?"

He said, "I heard you coming here; that's why I came here to see you." We shook hands. I gave him a huge hug and tapped him on his back. We had been talking about different things. Then he asked me how I knew that was him dressed in black down there on earth on the golf course at the Minerals Resort in Vernon, NJ. You see, he knew what I was thinking at that time where we met on the golf course. The answer is simple: he's Lord Jesus Christ.

I told him, "Who else would do that?" He wanted to be noticed; he knew that I would walk that way and that he was walking next to me, and simply, he jumped in front of me. He could do anything, I mean everything. He asked me if I liked the way he was dressed. I replied that I did like it and he looked cool.

The place looked just like jail in a daytime television room. Plus, they have a store with all different things. It's a rough place. Imagine if all your life you had been a good person, then you drove your car under the influence of alcohol, you got in an accident, and you killed someone. You would go there, and you would be with all those terrible criminals. This is only one example.

June 29, 2016

It was a beautiful sunny day. I got up in the morning of June 29, 2016, and decided to walk to the store to the next town, which is about twenty-five minutes each way. I walked by myself. Almost every morning I walk by myself. Most of the time I'm walking on the golf course. Sometimes I'm walking to the town, to the post office, to the library, or to the convenience store. I love walking.

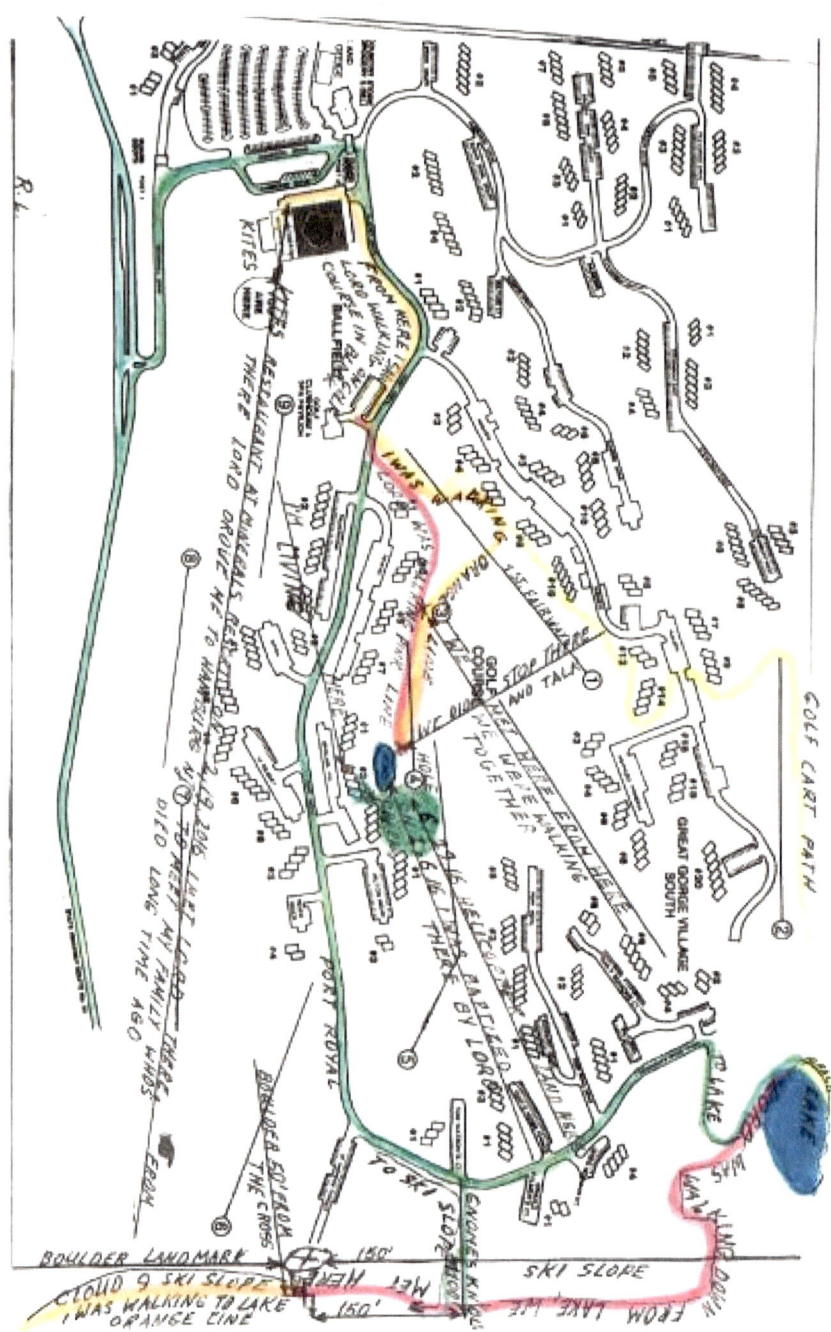

This map shows many points where a lot of miracles happened.

When I take the train to Penn Station, then I'm walking from there to Lincoln Center, all over Central Park. And then later afternoon, I was walking back to Penn Station, which is located on 8th Ave. and 33rd Street.

I went for a long walk on Route 94 in Vernon, NJ. While crossing a small bridge, I noticed the Lord standing there. I said hello to him, and he did the same. I didn't know why I didn't talk to him. Maybe he made me move forward because he knew my program for this day. It struck me that he wanted me to do something, that a major life event was about to unfold for me. There was something the Lord wanted me to do that day.

It was getting late when I got home. I took off my sweatshirt and I stepped out on the patio and hung up my shirt. When I came home, I noticed a yellow helicopter landed on the grass in front of my window about a hundred feet from my condominium. I thought to myself, What is this helicopter doing here? My neighbor and her friend were tanning by the pond.

She said to me, "What's this helicopter doing here?"

I said, "It's mine."

She said, "Yours?"

I replied, "It's mine."

I got on the helicopter, and we flew to New York City to a pier on 59th Street. I don't know how I got on the helicopter. I was unconscious (they made me be unconscious).

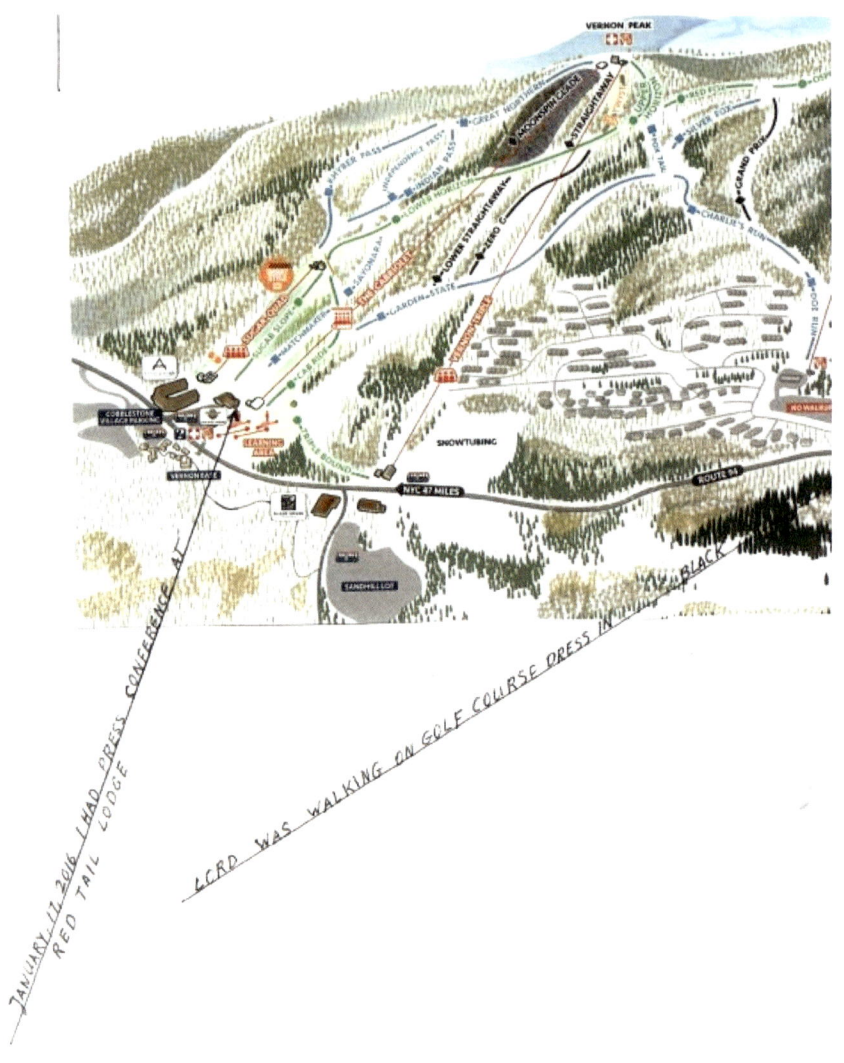

JANUARY 17 2016 I HAD PRESS CONFERENCE AT
RED TAIL LODGE

LCRD WAS WALKING ON GOLF COURSE DRESS IN ALL BLACK

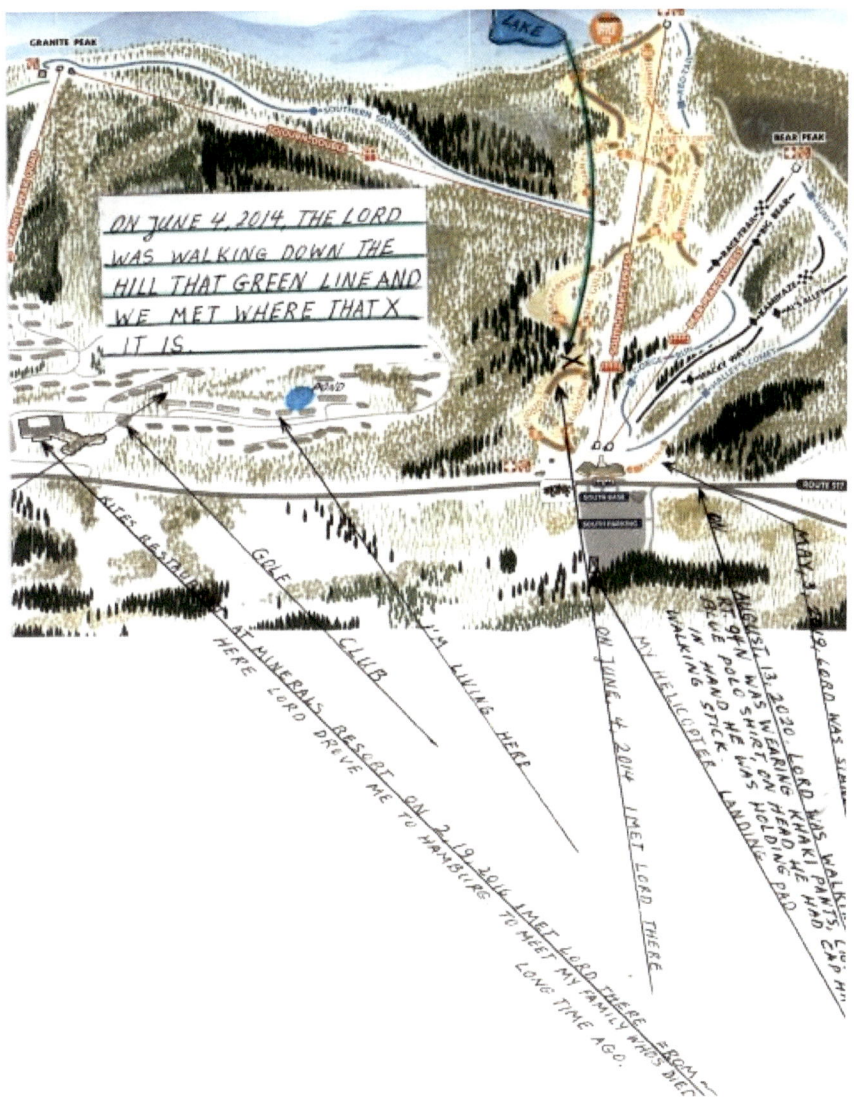

ON JUNE 4, 2014, THE LORD
WAS WALKING DOWN THE
HILL THAT GREEN LINE AND
WE MET WHERE THAT X
IT IS.

At the end of June 2016, I landed in this helicopter on Roosevelt Aircraft Carrier on the Virginia Coast.

On June 29, I landed on the Roosevelt Aircraft Carrier in a yellow helicopter, and the red Roosevelt Aircraft Carrier at the end of June 2016 on the Virginia Coast. From here I flew two helicopters on the Roosevelt Aircraft Carrier on the Virginia Coast.

On the helicopter, there were at least two of us, the pilot and me—but I know guardian angels, and of course, on a day like that, Lord Jesus Christ was with us.

I regained my semi-consciousness on Pier 59 in New York City. We were already late. Secret Service stopped the traffic, and there was so many of them—a few Suburbans, trucks, and agents all stopped the traffic. They put Little Angel and me in a stretch limousine and drove us to the Plaza Hotel. They took us to separate rooms, dressed her in a white skirt-suit and me also in a white suit. Agents were around the Plaza Hotel, and they put us back in the limousine. They stopped traffic again on 5th Ave. and drove us to St. Patrick's Cathedral for ceremony.

And today, the Cardinal was waiting for us, Little Angel and me, who was the mother of Ramona and Gabriela. Once we got in front of the Cardinal, he said, "This will be a simple ceremony at the cathedral because you are running late. You are going to meet presidents on the Roosevelt Aircraft Carrier." I told the Cardinal that the cathedral was so clean and the exterior was very shiny. He replied that I paid for that with $220,000,000 and also thanked me for it. I told him it was worth every penny. Little Angel and I were married by the Cardinal. We had a short ceremony, just as the Cardinal had promised.

I had been talking with the Cardinal at St. Patrick's Cathedral about delivering my letter to the pop about my experience seeing my family. The Cardinal told me the Vatican lent my money to an Italian developer, but he went bankrupt—we did get the money back. That was a big scandal. After that, Pope XVI resigned.

I asked him how he knew they were using my money, and he said that Cardinals and Popes are connected with a higher power. We were also talking about the Lord, and I told him he was standing next to us. He asked how I knew, and I said, "On a day like this, he is here."

Hudson River and Verrazano Bridge. Once we got in helicopters above the Hudson River, two F-16 arrived and after introduced themselves, escorted us to Roosevelt Aircraft Carrier on Virginia Coast.

After meeting with the Cardinal, we went back to the pier and onto my helicopter; another helicopter also joined us. Once we got above the Hudson River, two F-16s, fully armed, joined us. After introducing themselves, the pilots from those two F-16s informed me that we were flying to the Roosevelt Aircraft carrier off the Virginia coast. They also said the president was already on the aircraft carrier and he was waiting for me. I was truly shocked that all of this was happening, but I knew that I was being used in the service of the Lord.

Once we landed, those two F-16s circled the aircraft carrier a couple of times to make sure that everything was under control. The commander and seamen were onboard greeting me. To my shock, President Obama, President Putin, President Hollande, Chancellor Angela Merkel, First Lady Michelle Obama, and the Obama daughters were also on the carrier.

With his hands, President Obama asked those two pilots to make some flips, and they did.

After the ceremony, President Obama said to me, "You will have to debate with them, and he is going to sit and listen instead of debate." For some reason, I just knew they were asking me to debate foreign policy, and I had plans regarding the South China Sea. In five minutes, I put my plans on the table. They were plans about the South China Sea. China has had growing military

The Statue of Liberty.

The idea for the statue was born in 1865, when the French historian and abolitionist Edward de Laboulaye proposed a monument to commemorate the upcoming centennial of US independence (1876). Height from ground to torch 305 feet 1 inch (93 meters.)

National Immigration Museum Outdoor Tablet on Ellis Island.

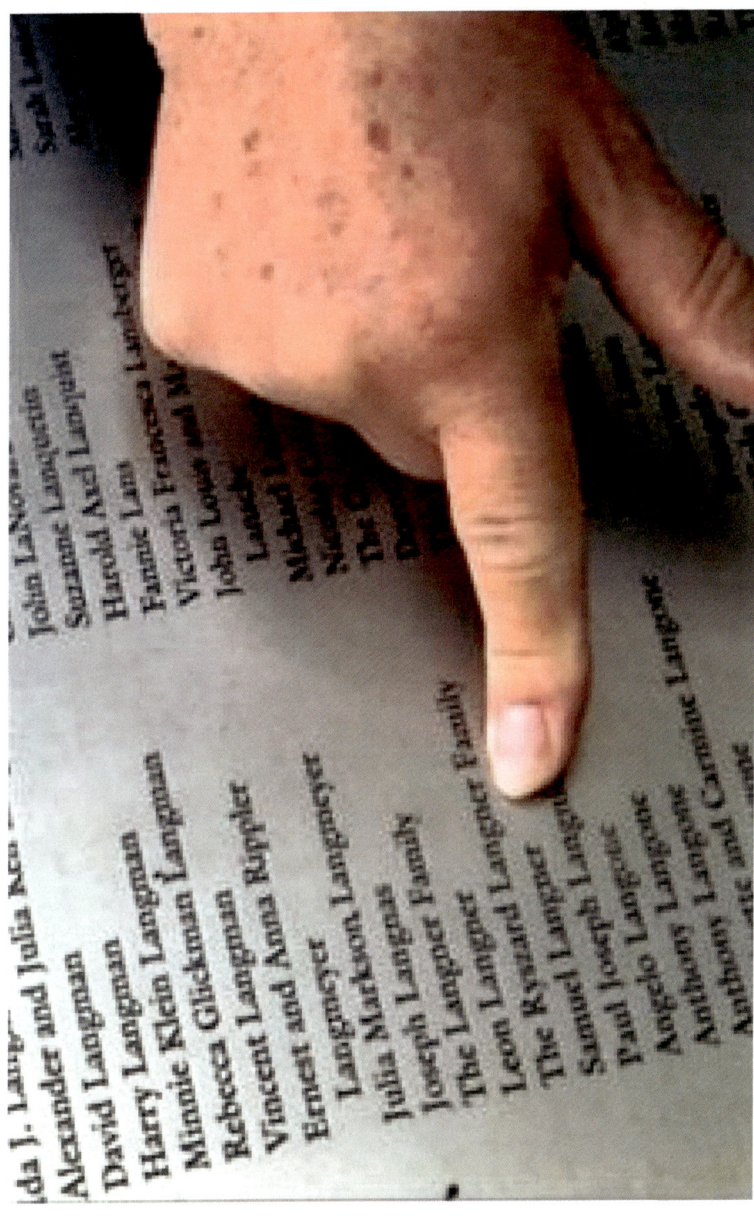

My name is on an outdoor tablet as the Ryszard Langner Family. Ryszard was my Polish first name. In 2016, president asked Ellis Wand museum authority to add to the tablet name "The Langner Family."

National Immigration Museum.

I had been registered in this museum in December 1970. Three months before I arrived in New York City. I arrived in New York City March 27, 1971.

These are two chestnuts that our Lord likes so much. The Lord was very upset when I said to Yvonka that she could dig out the smaller chestnut. These two chestnuts and those impassions are growing under that tall cedar tree. Pond is located on forward-left.

One of those flower baskets on out patio.

Every year we had this kind of flower baskets hanging on our patio. Baskets like that needs one small bucket of water and miracle grow. We are receiving a lot of compliments for our garden and those flowers growing there.

After I showed the direction to that bear, it walked behind that sign.

Bears are very often by this pond. Other animals too. Everyday we have Herons fishing in this pond.

In 2015 me and my wife we planted impassions flowers; under cedar tree and in the back of our corner condominium , front, and the end of the unit. Also we had few hanging baskets. Our condo it's located about 40' front pond, so I had been using water to water plants and flowers right from the pond. After I repeated few times my trip to the pond, on next one from pond, I have a big surprise. After I scooped water from the pond and after I got on the top of the pond bank and walking few feet, I asked myself? Did I saw anything walking behind me. I turned my head back and noticed huge black bear walking just behind me. I showed him with my arm the direction to the pond.

Trump Tower 721 5th Avenue New York City.

Empire State Building

Metropolitan Museum in New York City

Art Gallery in the Manhattan, New York City

power and they were building islands there. China was becoming a growing
danger to the rest of the world. It was time to stop them from building bases.

After relaying my plans to the presidents surrounding the table, I was chosen to lead that meeting. My plans were to send over navy ships into the South China Sea to stop them from breaking international laws. I needed the powerful leaders to support my plan to send US navy ships. The presidents and Chancellor agreed with me there. It was time to stop China from what they were doing in the South China Sea.

The president who was sitting on my right side turned his head slightly toward me and nodded his head yes. I did the same, along with President Hollande and the Chancellor. It seemed like everyone was in agreement that we would, collectively, send ships into the South China Sea. The time for immediate action was now.

I wanted the green light to send our ships to the South China Sea. Next, President Putin said to me, "Push the button, because you are the most powerful man in the world." Putin again said to push the button, and I did. I sent the message to those people who had an interest in that matter.

After my meeting on Roosevelt Aircraft Carrier in June 2016, international court in Haag in Holland, announced that China was illegally using international waters and building islands, and gave us the green light to move in and protect freedom of navigation in South China Sea. Ever since, there's been peace. I continued to work with politicians and leaders, and to give press conferences.

Back on the Roosevelt Aircraft Carrier, I spent more than three hours on the aircraft, so there was a lot of discussion. All the presidents wanted me to talk; they had me and they wanted to get as much as possible from me. I mentioned to Chancellor Angela Merkel that there's nothing better than getting good emigrants with diplomas and good skills. When they come to your country, they roll up their sleeves and go to work.

The president heard that and very quietly asked me if I rolled up my sleeves.

I replied, "My sleeves were always up. I had been working at a Polish coal mine for about seventy hours a week. When I had an auto business, I was working around a hundred hours." I went back to Angela Merkel, and we had the most interesting conversation. She's funny, she likes to talk and to ask questions. I said, "Chancellor..."

She said, "Yes?"

"You have to be very careful with that emigration because you could destabilize the European Union and the whole world."

She replied, "What do you suggest?"

I said, "Close the borders." She asked me how. I asked her, "What would you do if one million Turkish soldiers on horses with swords in their hands invaded your country?"

She replied, "I would send my army."

I said, "That's the way to do it."

Then she asked, "What about those existing?"

I said, "Put them on trains and send them back home. You must know who is coming to your home. It will be hard to spread them between European Union members. If you will send a million immigrants to small countries like Slovakia, you will change their culture." She took my advice and did what I advised her to do after there was so much crime and bombings. One day I will visit her.

She said to me, "You are an immigrant yourself, right?"

My answer was, "I will tell you how I emigrated. I was in Vienna, and after a while I decided to move to the United States. I went to the embassy in Vienna and I applied for a green card. That was in mid-September of 1970. By Christmas I got a letter from the Vienna embassy that I was approved for permanent residency in the United States. I got a visa, and on March 27, 1971, I was on my way to a new home in a new world. I arrived in the late afternoon; it was dark outside, I couldn't wait till the next day. I wanted to see Manhattan,

Broadway, and more. Probably the Lord was behind my back because everything went fast and smoothly."

President Obama asked me, "You had been waiting a long time for a visa. Was that the right way to do it?"

I replied, "That's the only way to do it."

The president added, "Did you arrive in the United States before Christmas 1970? If you did, you are registered on Ellis Island and your name is written on an outdoor tablet stand."

My name had been written "Ryszard Langner," my Polish name. In 2016 President Obama requested Ellis Island authority to put my new name, "Richard Langner and Family." Now I'm in two places. President Obama asked me if I had been to Ellis Island. I said I had not. After that meeting, I have been there a couple of times.

I went back to the president's question and I said, "I arrived on March 27, 1971. I was approved for permanent residency in the United States, before Christmas in 1970. See for yourself." They couldn't wait for me. Everyone sitting there had been laughing loudly.

The Chancellor asked me, "Were you impressed by New York City?"

"Yes, who wouldn't be impressed with New York City!"

Spring. Central Park in New York City is getting alive. Who wouldn't like
New York City, the greatest city in the world.

Central Park South art gallery.
Astro Gallery of Gems

Located in the heart of Manhattan New York City, the largest gem and mineral gallery in the world, suitable for both the novice as well as the advanced collector.

The New York Public Library, on Fifth Avenue. Behind the library it is Bryant Park. In the winter there is ice skating rink.

Plaza hotel in New York City. Located west of Fifth Avenue and is between 58th street and central park south.

Rockefeller Center in the midtown Manhattan, New York City.

Rockefeller center is famous for its annual tree lighting, also in the winter there is ice skating rink. I had been ice skating there many times in the mid-1970s.

Times Square in New York City, on every New Year, that ball on top of the roof. It's dropped every New Year Eve since 1904.

Radio City Music Hall in New York City

The Vessel

Central Park in New York City

Central Park is an urban park between the Upper Westside and Upper East Side neighborhoods in Manhattan in New York City. Cherry Blossoms April 6, 2023.

Lincoln Center

Lincoln Center for the performing arts.

Carriages in Central Park

Central Park in New York City, there is many attractions; there is the zoo, lake with boats in winter ice skating rink and more.

Grand Central Terminal in Manhattan New York City." Below: "Grand Central Terminal is one of the worlds ten more visited tourist attractions with 21.6 million visitors in 2018, excluding train and subway passengers.

World Trade Center, view from Hudson River

"Little Island at Pier 55"

I was at a hotel on 27th and 5th Avenue for over a few days. I told her the weather was bad, windy, and cold, so those first few days I didn't really enjoy. Besides, there were so many important things on my mind, like how to find a job and an apartment. The next day I went to the social security office to get my card. When you are twenty-four years old, everything is funny and challenging, especially when you have the Lord behind your back.

That evening a young man came up to my hotel to meet with me. He was writing to Polish American daily news and his name was Edward. After he introduced himself, he presented his plans to me. That evening he took me to Jersey City, which was only twenty minutes away by subway, to meet with his friends. The next afternoon, my new friend, Marian, took me with him to his work, where he was working the second shift. After he introduced me to his boss, his boss said, "You're starting immediately." I had been dressed like I would go to Church.

I said, "I don't have any work clothes."

He said, "You won't get dirty; you are going to Johnson and Johnson to clean lights inside offices. We have some old sneakers you could wear today. Hurry up, because that van is waiting!" After all, I had my first job.

I had good conversation on aircraft carrier with the Chancellor and presidents and Putin: BO, FH, VP. They like to hear from me as much as possible, and they kept asking questions, and I was more than happy to tell them any stories. I told them one of my experiences with a bear. Since I'm living in the bear country, I had many accounts with them.

I thought about the summer of 2015, when I planted impassions flowers under a cedar tree. That tree is about fifty feet high. It's growing on the end of the right side of my huge window. This window is twelve feet wide. On the left side of my window, I have a patio. In front of my window is a nice-sized pond, which is about forty feet from my window. The summer of 2015 was very hot and dry, so I needed to water my flowers growing under that tree and in hanging baskets every day. I gave them plenty of water, and I fertilized them too, so I had nice flowers and I got a lot of my neighbors and golfers because on the end of the pond is the fifth hole. So when they stop there they have time to look around. Usually, I took my watering bucket from my patio, went to the pond. I scooped water and I went to water the flowers hanging in baskets. I went back and I did the same thing: scooped water.

At Botanical Garden Orchid Show

E. H. conservatory is a greenhouse at New York Botanical Gardens." Below: "New York Botanical Garden one of the leading centers of Botanical research in the United States. The 250 acre garden, located in Bronx Park, New York City has a plant collection consisting of about 12,000 species from almost every plant of the world.

T. Tower 721 5th Avenue Manhattan, New York City. On January 9, 2017, I had meeting at T. Tower with D. family, I had been instructed about my future duty at The White House. Also Yvona gave me tour through my new condominium which she beautifully decorated for me.

When I had been walking towards my patio, I thought to myself, Did I just see someone behind me? After that, I thought I did, so I turned my head back and I saw a huge bear walking behind me about five feet away. Without any panic I showed him with my arm, the direction to walk to the pond, and when I showed it to him, I made the sound with my mouth, "Shooo." To my surprise, that bear walked exactly in that direction that I showed him to walk. Then I walked to my patio. I sat on my patio and watched him. After he saw me sitting, he walked up, because the pond was a little lower than the area around. First, he was walking, then he was slowly running away.

Everyone was very excited with my story. Like always, Angela had a lot of questions and I needed to show her how that bear was moving by that pond because that bear was very nervous. Someone was holding him there and then saw me sitting on the patio.

After meeting on the Roosevelt Aircraft Carrier, when everyone left, I was still talking to the president. The president said to me, "I have been sitting and listening to you talking; you remind me of President Ronald Reagan. You are not taking no for an answer." Then he added that I would be a good president. I replied that I probably would be. "There is a loophole," he said. "If someone lives here more than forty-four years, you could run for the president's office."

After the meeting had ended, I found myself at dinner with the Obamas, Presidents VP, FH, and Chancellor AM. Then, after dinner, I handed each of them medals to commemorate the meeting, minted especially for that occasion. I also received many, many medals. President Obama said nobody had ever received that many medals and nobody ever will. The most valuable medal I received from President Obama was the Purple Heart.

The first medal I handed out was to Michelle, then Malia, then Sasha, and next, the president. An invisible person told me to give medals to the president's daughters. I believe it was my guardian angel speaking. I had enough for them. I had seven, but not for myself, and for someone? So, we ordered two more, one for me and one for someone.

I went to Malia, and she said to me, "Me too."

I assumed that she was shocked that she also got a medal too; she wanted a medal, and that she wanted to spend time with us. I said to her, "You are here. You are with us. You are keeping us company."

Then I went to Sasha, and she said to me, "Me too."

I said, "But of course. Nobody will go home empty handed."

Next, I gave a medal to the president. The medals were to commemorate that special meeting, our relationship, and our friendship. Those medals that they received from me are collector's items; only nine were minted for that occasion to commemorate that meeting.

I also asked him if he could use the briefcase in which I had delivered documents of the defense system to him.

He said, "Just say it."

I said, "Mr. President, could you use this briefcase after all of the documents are removed?"

When I said to the president, "Mr.," he said, "Don't call me 'Mr.', call me 'Barak Obama.'" After I handed him the briefcase with the documents, the president gave me ranks: "Honor admiral" and "Five Star General." After I received those medals, the president said they are going to put me in the Guinness Book of World Records!

The president said, "I accept this gift. Those two items will be the most valuable items in my library." That briefcase was made from seal leather. It was waterproof, with a compartment and balloon, which works like airbags in cars, like my patent for airplanes when they crash into oceans or other places. That would make it easy to find them.

There were others at the dinner, and they also received medals from me. We had a great conversation as I handed around the medals. Next were President Holland, the Chancellor, and the president. The president asked me to call him Vlad. I said, "Call me Rich."

The Chancellor said, "You gave away all of the medals, and you don't have any for yourself."

I responded, "That's all right. I will go the president's library to see them."

I shared my experience I had in Thessaloniki, Greece, in the summer of 1977 with the Chancellor, President Holland, and Putin.

First, I flew from New York to London, England. From there I flew to Istanbul, Turkey. After a few days of site seeing historical Istanbul, I went by train to Thessaloniki in Greece. The distance from Istanbul to Thessaloniki is three hundred kilometers, less than two hundred miles. That was some experience. It took me thirty hours to get to my destination. The train stopped so many times in the middle of nowhere; people got out of the train after the conductor announced that this train would be stopping there for thirty minutes or more. That happened a few times. For domestic people that was normal.

Once I got to Thessaloniki, my mood changed. Thessaloniki is located by sea. It's a modern city and a tourist destination. I really enjoyed myself in this nice city. On my last day of staying in Thessaloniki, after all day on tours, I got to my hotel. I went to my room to refresh myself, then I went downstairs to the restaurant for dinner. I spent about ninety minutes eating my dinner. After I paid, I stepped outside and crossed the street. I was walking on the sidewalk by the sea. I walked for about five minutes, enjoying my walk and views. It was dark, but all those lights reflecting off the water made a nice picture.

At one moment, that picture changed. I heard loud noises; it was roaring and I couldn't walk. I felt like I was on a boat on the ocean with huge waves. First, I thought to myself, Bomb exploded! But in a split second, I came to the conclusion that it was an earthquake, very strong, seven on the Richter scale. That earthquake lasted only a few seconds, but that was enough time for me to remind myself of earthquakes in Shopie, in former Yugoslavia, Nicaragua, where the earth was cracking wide open and people were falling in.

I was walking about one quarter of a mile when I spotted a small park with small trees and branches. I decided to go there. I saw at that square a delicatessen, so I went in and asked for a bottle of Coca-Cola. The owner of that store told me to get out because there will be aftershock. I asked him again, and once again he said to get out. I knew that I was going to spend the night in the park and I would be thirsty. I asked him one more time and this time he sold it to me.

I had been all set for the night at the park. There were a lot of people at the park. That night I met Polish workers who were transporting sheep from Poland to Libya. They were feeding them while transporting them. I spent all night talking with them.

In the morning I went back to my hotel to pack my clothes because I had an early flight to Frankfurt in Germany. Once I got to the hotel, I noticed broken glass on the floor. The building was shaking again, and the worker at that hotel told me to get out. I said to him that I have to take my stuff because I had a flight in the morning. I said to myself, I'm going to just pack my stuff quickly and I will leave. There was no shaking for a while, so I decided to have a very quick shave, but once I started, there was aftershock. I stopped shaving, and was a bit scared, but I continued and finished. I packed my stuff, and I left. I took a taxi to the airport and saw that it also had a lot of damage.

I told the Chancellor and presidents that I had been happy and had a nice experience. The Chancellor asked me, "Why?"

I replied, "Because nothing happened to me, and now I know how that feels."

The Chancellor on the aircraft carrier said to me, "And you kept that secret from the Commander-in-Chief?"

I said, "These are secret defense systems which I wanted to deliver myself."

After that, the president started praising me. He said that I always put someone in front myself; there was always someone more important than himself. Then he said that I have a trillion dollars in my account in the Treasury Department, but maybe more, because that statement came two weeks ago. He also said that twice, in a single day, one billion dollars went to the treasury from one man to my account.

Then each president invited me to his or her country. President Putin said to just email him when I wanted to come to Russia and he would send his private plane to pick me up.

Vlad asked me, "Do you know how to ride a horse?" I said no; he said, "We will teach you." (George W. told me at the White House on January 20, 2017, that President Putin is very good on a horse. He and Putin were riding at Camp David. George added that they would teach me.) Never before did I see the president wearing a chain with a cross on his neck. Not long ago I saw him on TV and I saw him wearing a heavy chain and a big cross on it. I liked that Vlad. Vlad said to me, "Send me your email address when you want to come visit me. Then I will send my personal private plane to pick you up." He said the plane would be parked at the airport, "You just fly your helicopter and land next to it, get on, and you'll be on your way. You won't have to go through all the chaos."

President Hollande said that he would like to have me for a state dinner. The Chancellor also invited me to Germany. After all of this, NBC interviewed me on the Roosevelt Aircraft Carrier. It was a relatively short interview but got the point across of everything that had happened at the meeting.

MSNBC asked me, "Sir, how did you make that kind of fortune?"

I said, "Maybe the president will answer better than me."

President Obama said, "I will." He turned his head left, right, and left again, and said, "He has more patents than I have hair on my head."

I said, "You have a lot of hair on your head."

He said, "That's the point."

I stepped in and said, "I'm not done." I still had more patents to file.

"He is not done yet," agreed the president.

Doing interviews had become fairly commonplace for me. After that miracle at the hospital, and after the press conference at Red Tail Lodge, I was on the front page of every newspaper around the world. Reporters at that time knew everything about me. They asked me about my patents, which was my main way of making money. My first patent was a beach umbrella that could be screwed into the sand. I described this patent to Nicole Wall when she asked about it, and several of the presidents overheard.

The Chancellor, in particular, asked me how I got that idea. I told her I had been sitting on a beach on a very windy day and I saw umbrellas flying all over and people struggling with them. I thought to myself, Wouldn't it be so much easier if umbrellas just screwed in the sand?

After the Chancellor and the other presidents left, I was still talking with president and his wife about different things. We were talking about my patents and about foreign policy goals.

The president was in shock. He told me he had been to meetings like the G7, G-20, and others, but world leaders could not accomplish anything at those meetings. He said he hadn't seen anything like that level of immediate cooperation among the world leaders. "They just fell in love with you." He said he had been at all kinds of meetings and couldn't get any agreements. He couldn't get anything done. Those were his words.

I said, "Sometimes, we just quickly get to the right spot in someone's brain." I knew that my skill in convincing people was a gift from the Lord.

Between the combination of my miracles, meetings with the presidents, and time spent on the front page of newspapers, I was extremely famous. People not only wanted to meet with me and spend time with me, but many famous women wanted to marry me. I told them I was married, happily married, and that I was also a father.

I became a father a second time in July of 2016, when my second daughter was born. Her name is Gabriela. Little Angel chose the name Gabriela for our daughter by herself because she knew that I loved that name. Once again I was shocked, because I didn't know she was pregnant. I don't see them on a daily basis. They are angels, invisible.

On July 4, 2016, two F-16s were flying above my condominium; they flew overhead a few times. Each time they flew the condominium building was shaking. I believe they did that to say thanks to me for what I did that June for our country.

In the summer of 2016, the man paid for my cognac; he said God doesn't pay. Then he asked me to bless him because he is bad. He asked me what the Lord was going to do. I told him, "When the time comes, I will remember you." He still wanted me to bless him then. He sounded like he committed terrible crimes.

October 18, 2016

On October 18, 2016, the Lord and a little angel thought that they would stop me from contacting the Cardinal; the little angel told me that. They committed a terrible mistake on that day. But I still contacted the Cardinal; I needed to inform him of everything that had been happening. I needed to tell the Cardinal that I had been in contact with the Lord frequently and that the Lord and Little Angel did something not right.

October 26, 2016, T TOWER

At the tower I was hosting a historic meeting with the presidential candidates. I was having a press conference at the tower with presidential candidates D.T. and H.C. The 2016 election season was in high gear at this point, so journalists and campaigns were consulting me frequently. This meeting was no different; there were many high-profile politicians and journalists present. Also present were B, the Cardinal, the Cardinal's mother, the New York mayor, MC, MK, and other reporters from around the world. That was a productive night.

I flew a helicopter to New York City from Vernon, where I was living, and one of my helicopters was in a park at daytime. Every night it's moved to the airport—Taterboro Airport. I flew to Pier 59 in New York City. From there, a limo drove me to Tower, 721 Fifth Avenue. When I got there, everybody was waiting for me. I ran in and everybody was clapping their hands, so I did the same thing.

I opened up the evening by saying, "Good evening, ladies and gentlemen. It's an honor to be with you all here tonight. Presidential candidates are going to ask questions instead of me asking them questions."

The reporter asked me, "Are you going to South China Sea? What did you do with those ships?"

I asked her, "What ships?"

She said, "Those in the South China Sea."

I said, "You mean those fishing boats?" She said yes. I said, "I don't know what's happened with those fishing boats. I assumed when our ships got there they pushed them aside between those rocks." All of the people in the conference room were loudly laughing, including the Cardinal. (The next day, I was on the front page of every newspaper around the world. The president told me China was furious. Bill C would be talking about this at the White House on January 20, 2017, on Inauguration Day.)

Then she asked me about the president of the Philippines, who turned his back at us, after we did so much work to keep peace at South China Sea. I was joking that I think I heard he was arrested and he's in jail. Once again, people were laughing.

Also, she asked me, "What's going to happen with the South China Sea?"

I said, "China is a civilized country and respects all international laws. China owns only two hundred miles of sea in South China Sea."

"How about Philippines?"

"Philippines owns exactly the same."

"What are you going to do with the rest of that sea?"

"The rest is international waterways; it is and will be of use for free navigation, and above it is the airline corridor."

A reporter then asked me how long I'm going to live. I said, "When I was born, they gave me ninety-six years, but they changed their minds."

The reporter asked me again, "So how long are you going to live now?"

I said, "I don't know if I can tell you that, but I will tell you that I'm not going to die."

The Cardinal was at this conference, and upon hearing that I would never die, he called someone to go to the cathedral for Holy Water. After the Holy Water was brought, the Cardinal washed my feet. He came to me, asked me to sit on the floor, to take my shoes and socks off, and he was ready to wash my feet. Before he washed my feet, I didn't want him to, but he said, "That's how this is supposed to be done in this situation." YES, that was at. Records are at every media archive.

Later that night, DT announced that he gave me a condominium at T Tower on 5th Avenue with a 360-degree view. He said, "Just go to the front desk, show them your ID, and they will give you the key." I couldn't believe my fortune; but, then again, I had been very helpful to during his campaign, and of course, he would want to thank me properly.

At the end M came to me and asked if I liked her haircut now. I didn't like it when her hair was covering her eye. She said, "Thank you for sending me the beautician from Paris on private jet. You love me."

I said, "I like you very much."

She replied, "No, no, no, no, you sent me a beautician from Paris on private jet. Say you love me."

"I almost love you."

HRC overheard our conversation and yelled, "Nobody sends a beautician from Paris on a private jet to me!"

Mark was standing next to me and asked me, "How much did that cost? Who paid for that?"

I said, "Someone did."

After the press conference, MK, MC, the Cardinal, and I went for a cock-tail hour. MK asked me if I was going to eat, and I said yes. She said she was going to make a nice platter for herself and me and then asked if I was on a diet because I'm so skinny. She also asked me if I was going to stay for dinner. I said, "No, she's going to sit next to me."

A beautician from Paris has a business on 57th Street and 5th Avenue. Bill C. likes her, and is going to her for a haircut. HC said thanks to me for finding a good designer for her. I didn't like the way she was dressed while she had been campaigning. There is nothing better than to make someone happy. How I know all of them, because all of them once knew me. Mark told me, "I'm not just here as the richest man in the world because I'm not from here, I'm from there, and I don't count." I assume he meant that I'm from up above. Many famous people had their hair done at the beautician from Paris's place, MK, and I believe she does all their famous friends.

I was talking to the candidates and DT. I said, "Ladies first," started this way. Each candidate wanted my support. I asked them to ask me questions first. She said, "I know it's up to you who will be the next president. You can make history, or you can destroy history. Never in our history was a woman so close to becoming president of the United States of America."

She asked me, "What do you want me to do? Get on my knees, or do you want me to cry?"

I said, "I don't want you to cry or get on your knees. Just keep campaigning." She said if she wins, I would be in her administration.

At the end, she said to me, "Think about it." She believed that, with my help, she would be able to win. Maybe she was right.

Then I went to D.T. and praised him and his family.

She overheard me praising his family and asked, "What about my family?"

I said, "I don't know why I didn't say anything about your family." I praised her for being in public service for thirty years, and I also praised her husband, a former president, for being a very successful president. I also praised her daughter and her children.

After that, I went back to. said, "Ten Einsteins won't equal him." Then he said, "Nobody ever before in the world flew two helicopters and was escorted by two F-16s fully armed."

Also, he announced that he gave me a condominium at on Fifth Ave in New York City with a 360-degree view. He also said when he is elected president, he would be president, but "Rich is going to run this country."

Also, he said that I complained that my condo was too small, and it was hard for me to work, and I didn't have any room in my closets. He said he gave me a condominium and was decorating it for me. He said, "We are going to hire employees and do a lot of inventing and we will make a ton of money." He said I could only be supervisor.

RC came up and asked me who assigned over two F-16s. I said, "I don't know who assigned them, but I can tell you I was carrying secret defense systems in my briefcase that are my patent and gift to our country."

After that, someone pulled a string from a balloon which was hanging from the ceiling, and ten million dollars flew down on the floor. That was my campaign donation.

After that I said to the Cardinal, "It's nice seeing you again."

He replied, "It's nice seeing you too." Then he pointed at his mother, who was sitting next to him, and I said hello.

Then I said to the mayor of New York City, "I think those horses and carriages should stay in the city because they are tourist attractions and a city decoration."

DT said, "Rich, don't worry, they are not going anywhere."

The mayor said it's dangerous. I told him that in Warsaw, and Krakow, and in Polish City they have them. In the summer of 2016, the Cardinal was in historical Krakow and really liked horses and carriages. He also liked Church Mariacki, in the center of the city, with the Black Madonna.

from Fox News said to me, "Rich, let's write the book about miracles at the hospital, the press conference at Red Tail lodge, what happened on June 29, 2016, and the whole day on the aircraft. We can make a billion dollars."

The next day I had been in front of every newspaper around the world. Also, that day I was on every news channel. My nephew in Germany was taking pictures of the TV. Also, the next day, he bought newspapers and clipped out the articles and pictures. I was the most holy man in that space.

After I wrote to MK and said, "Let's do it," someone went to her and said if she were to write the book, they would destroy her. I believe that person was my Lord's negotiator. The Lord doesn't want this true story to be published.

I had a meeting with the president and his family at the T. Tower. The president told me that I'm going to live in Washington and work with him. He also told me that I'm going to give a speech at the White House on Inauguration Day. I said, "I'm not a good speaker." DT said that it would be a short speech. He seemed to know everything that was going to happen that night. He also said that MK said that I'm a better speaker than him. Next, the former president asked me about his administration they chose. I was one of them. He asked me why I chose RT. I replied, "Because he is businessman and also he is a politician." RT was working for a big oil company; he was engineer and energy executive. He knew all the executives around the world, with whom he met and made very important decision and deals. Also he met with the King of Saudi Arabia. The president of Russia and other leaders of the world which their countries produce oil. That's why I choose him as (secretary) 69 US secretary of state. He took the office of secretary of state on February 1, 2017. He lasted only one year and two months. He was a very intelligent person and businessman. The former president didn't like anyone constantly correcting him and teaching him. Finally, he was fired by DJT on March 13, 2018, also on January 9, 2017, at that meeting former president asked me why I don't like RG to be the sixty-ninth secretary of the state. I reply RG is good. He was famous mayor of New York City. He served as mayor of New York City from 1994–2001; he was a businessman, attorney, and politician. But I said to the former president, "I don't see him as the secretary of state. I only saw him as the city politician." And that's how RWT was chosen to be the sixty-ninth secretary of state.

IT asked me why I changed her first name from I to Yvanka. I said I made a mistake and after I realized it; the letter was already gone. She said she was laughing at first, but then she thought about it, and she came to the conclusion what her first name should be. I asked her, "Are you going to change your first name?"

She replied, "You already did. Why did you?"

On January 20. 2017 I had meeting with President Donald J. Trump at this office.

On January 20, 2017, Presidential Inauguration Day. D.J.T. it's swear

I said, "My former girlfriend had that name, which was spelled that way."

She added, "I like that, it should be like this." I was happy already that I did something good and I made YT happy.

Then, the president instructed me about my future job, told me where I was going to live, about my clothes, about the cleaners I was going to pick up my clothes from and things like that.

On that night, I was instructed about my future duties, which would be at in the president's administration. The was long list of my future duties, like briefing the president daily what was going on in the country and abroad. Making plans with JK for the president's future meetings, and his daily program. Also meeting abroad with politicians especially from peaceful countries, whom I already knew and debated with in the past. President DJT knew that I was very successful in the past debating with presidents and Chancellor on Roosevelt Aircraft Carrier on the Virginia coast on June of 2016. President DJT knew I would be very helpful to him and his administration. That's why he wanted me to be his advisor. I was very happy with the president's proposition, which I accepted without any hesitation. I did accept that job. I am business-man, entrepreneur, and I do like to be very active, creative, and this job offered me that life in the Washington, DC, and work with the president and other advisors, meeting with all those politicians from around the world. What was the most important thing to me was to work and to build better yet my beloved country, United States of America. That was my dream. I had my plans; I had been preparing myself for my new job. Also, I was getting ready to move to Washington, DC. My penthouse at former post office in the Washington, DC, on Pennsylvania Avenue was ready. Its location is only few blocks from the White House. It was ready and waiting for me. All my suits and all clothes were already in the closets. I.T. did good job, just like her father said at T Tower, she has a good eye. No one would do that better. Everything was done and was complete and just waiting for me. And I had been ready too, and very excited. I couldn't wait to move to my new quarter in the Washington, DC. I was living in Vernon, New Jersey, a small town in the mountains with many resorts. It's a very beautiful, quiet area. I also like big cities, city life, pulse and city rhythm. That job did offer me all that and more. I couldn't wait to move there and enjoy my life to the fullest. But my higher authority saw things far ahead. And they knew what was coming and what would happen with DJT and his administration. There was one scandal after another. One chaos after another. My higher authority didn't want me to work in that kind of environ-ment. After everything was set for me, my higher authority they made deci-sions that it would be better if I advised the president DJT from my home, and through my negotiator, coordinator. At first I was shocked and dis-appointed, but in the end I was happy about their decision. They see things always very far forward, and once again they were right. We all remember what's happened on January 6, 2021, in the Washington, DC.

The White House

DJT was furious when he found out that I was not coming to Washington, DC, to work with him side by side. I.T. was really very upset. After the inauguration, the president made a small change and I was supposed to work with I.T. instead of JK and advise her father. She was very happy that we would work together to advise the president. The president still wasn't happy that I wasn't at the White House close to him. He knew what I'd done in five minutes. On the Roosevelt Aircraft Carrier. That's why he wanted me to be in Washington. That's why I had on February 15, 2017, a meeting with I.T. at the T Tower to smooth things out. I did smooth things out. I almost got married to the president's daughter. But the higher authority didn't want this to happened and made me move out from Vernon and from Sussex County. Because after that would be the end of the world. That's why they couldn't let me move to Washington to live there and work with the president. That's why they are holding key and the deed to my condo at T Tower. I know that from my guardian angels and from Cardinal J.D. of New York. He had been told by my negotiator-coordinator (Lord's and my negotiator and coordinator). I'm very sure how things are set around me. The Lord came here with army of angels to protect me, and to prepare me for something big. I know that. Once the Lord asked me, "Did you notice the difference in your life after they came to protect you?" I replied, "Absolutely. My life did a 180." On November 12, 2012, an angel came to my office while I was eating my lunch and said to me,

"We came here to destroy you because you want work with us." We had plans to move to Florida; we sold our house, and the state was supposed to buy our garage because they were reconstructing Rt. 23 and they needed our property. My angels couldn't let this happened. So they need me to work with them. They had their plans, and they were moving with them very fast. On February 1, 2015, at St. Francis de Sales Catholic Church in Vernon, I was holding the Lord's hand while praying. We are on film on the Church's camera. Also in Cardinal TD's possession. One week later, on February 8, 2015, I held the hand of St. Pope John Paul II. At the same Church, with the Lord sitting few rows in front of us. After we finished the praying, he squeezed my hand very hard. The Lord did the same when we prayed. St. Pope John Paul II is a saint, he is in heaven, someone powerful sent him here to this Church on that mission to do that job. Who could do that? Someone more powerful than him. I believe that one could be our God himself. On September 10, 2014, my guardian angel, mother of two our daughters, came to my condominium, and she told me about my future. She said to me, "You don't know who you are," then she added "God is old and he needs your help." From my long experiences. I came to conclusion that there are two great powers which are working somehow together. Each party wants me to be on their side. One party came here to destroy me and force me to work with them and they are doing anything to succeed. The other party is directing me into direction I want to be. Since I was born, I have been with God. And I will stay this way forever. The first group wants to hold me through all kinds of manipulation (my guardian just kicked when I did wrote the word manipulation, which means yes). God gave me the option, and a simple choice, just to move out. This could happen soon. God can't wait forever. What I wrote is all true; most of the stories are in archives and in private hands. I still have a ton of true stories to share. Maybe in the next book.

Inauguration ball at the White House on January 20, 2017

President DT instructed me that I was to work with his son-in-law, JK, said by side, in the same office, "Two is always better than one," to prepare and advise president on a daily basis, make plans for the president's future meetings with world leaders, and all his daily duties. Also, I was supposed to meet with world leaders I already knew. In the end of January 2017 they called me and informed me that me and her will fly to Moscow to meet with president of Russia, whom I already knew well. Then she informed me that I was going to have my own office and she would be my secretary. I was very happy from that proposal, that I will be able to help president run this country and world. I had some experience with meeting world leaders and successfully debating with them. The former president did like my last debate with presidents and Chancellor on the Roosevelt Aircraft Carrier. He knew I would be of good help to him. But then my high authority didn't want me to be in the Washington and working with the president. Instead, I advised him from New Jersey. Everyone was disappointed, especially my future secretary, but my higher authority always see things far ahead and they knew and they saw what's coming. The former president did not always take good advice, from his good and loyal advisors. He many times said, "I'm the president not them—advisers." DJT was whole his life his own boss, and he didn't like anyone telling him what to do and what decision to make. DJT did a lot of good things and a lot good changes. But he lost reelection.

What really shocked me was when, in the beginning of the conversation, just like that, he said, "Rich is going to pay for the wall."

I said, "I'm not going to pay for the wall. I do have other responsibilities."

He asked, "What do you have other than building walls?"

I said, "For example, I just paid $220,000,000 for the renovation of St. Patrick's Cathedral." He knew how much money a day was coming into my account.

That night, after her father told her to do so, she gave me a tour inside my condominium, which was nice. He wasn't too happy with that. He said we could all go, but the president said it would be better if she would go there by herself because that would be too much of a distraction, and he was right. So, I went there, and she showed me around. She bought furniture and nicely decorated it. She said, "No one in my family is drinking except for me." She continued to say, "For what you have done for us, you will celebrate all holidays with us, and I will have a partner to drink with."

She started then to ask me very personal questions.

I said, "I don't want any problems here."

She said, "What problems? We are both adults, we can do whatever we want." We were talking for a long time. She is very sweet and a smooth talker.

Before we knew it, he got nervous and came up to see what was going on. He saw the way she was talking to me and looking at me. When we got back to the family, he asked me if I could heal his grandmother. I asked him how old she was, and I believe he said she was around ninety.

I said, "That's a nice age. We can't heal everyone. We are born to die."

He replied, "But you aren't going to die."

After she heard that, I.T. jumped in and asked me, "How about your wife?"

I answered, "I don't know." JK wasn't too happy that I didn't want to heal his grandma. He doesn't know that if you are a good person here, you will live better there than be old, sick, and suffering here. You get what you earn here, no more, no less. Then be a good human being, and remember, there is Heaven, Purgatory, and Hell. No one wants to go there, to Hell, believe me. I met people who were waiting to be judged, they know what Hell is. I have been there above, and I have talked with people who committed terrible crimes. They are really scared.

IT said, "I don't want to die."

Also, she told me that the condominium was in my name. A few weeks later, I wanted to use the condominium, so I did what they told me to do. After I showed the front desk my ID, they said, "We don't see anything in your name."

I said, "My negotiator had been doing all of the negotiating; that's why I don't have the deed and key in my possession. I have to be registered at city hall." They asked me who my negotiator is. "He was sent here to be my organizer. The Cardinal met him a few times." In my opinion, my negotiator was holding my deed and the key to my unit.

Since then, I have had many meetings with and other politicians and powerful people. I know that my job is to lead this country, and I do so with the help of the Lord and my guardian angels.

How I got to that meeting and back to Vernon, NJ, to my condominium, I don't know. For this you would have to ask our Lord. Just the same way to the Vatican in 2016 to deliver the letter to Pope Francis.

In the late afternoon, I flew a helicopter from Vernon, NJ, to Washington, DC. After I landed, Secret Service picked me up and drove me to the White House. After a few minutes there, a woman got on her knee in front of me with a huge diamond ring and asked me, "Would you marry me?" I said, "I'm married," and lifted her up. One man said, "Look! A woman is on her knee." For the first time I saw a woman on her knee. I wonder what he is going to say.

I was at the White House for a party. The president asked people on the dance floor to open up the center because "Rich will start the party with his dance." I started the dance with my partner, my guardian angel. People applauded; we got a lot of compliments, and I was also asked if I would like to be on Dancing with the Stars with other celebrities, who were also at the party.

While walking on the dance floor I met the First Lady once again and congratulated her for becoming the First Lady. She said I did that on January 9, 2017. I told her, but today it was official and it's at the White House. I added, "You should be very proud of yourself. You were a model and now you are the First Lady."

I was really surprised when she replied, "Rich, no, no, no, I'm not happy. I like a simple life." She started talking about college, her major being architecture. I told her that I love old architecture, and she said she did too. I added that I like Europe, cities like Vienna, Krakow, Istanbul, and those small towns in Europe. "We have a lot in common," she added. "I like that too. That was the reason that I took architecture." She didn't graduate because she became a model. Then we were talking about her work, modeling. Modeling is hard work. Since we had a lot in common, we could sit and talk forever.

She said to me, "Rich, you have one trillion two hundred billion dollars in your account in the treasury; you don't need this job. Rich, you won't be able to work with him, you are so intelligent and he's so controlling." I'm not living in Washington, DC, I'm living in Vernon, New Jersey, but I'm constantly advising President J. The president and First Lady are taking my advice.

She was right; I added two hundred billion dollars in six months. Two years later, I believe I'm worth more than two trillion. One day, I will be able to use all of that money. But money doesn't really mean anything to me. My experiences and my relationships are more important. Someday, I'm going to publish my story as a book and make a movie out of it—that's what matters to me: telling people my story.

Then first lady MT said to me, "Rich, how about me and you one day travel to Europe to visit cities like Krakow, Vienna, Paris, Rome, Slovenia, and other countries in the Europe, since we both like old architecture." I agreed with her. I said that's a good idea and I added that I was going to think about it and maybe one day in the future, when we will have some time for that long travel trip, we could make plan for that kind trip. I would like to see Slovenia. I did hear Slovenia is a beautiful country; it's located on border of Italy and Austria. Also, the First Lady was born there. A lot of polish people every year spending their vacation there, and they are happy of their choice. Slovenia is small country located in the southeastern Europe. It is a constitution republic of Yugoslavia, population 2,100,000 (estimated in 2015). The official language is Sloven. And its capital is Ljubljana MT, just like myself, loves to travel. She was in Poland and she visited the old historical Krakow and has good memories from that trip. That's why she would like to repeat that. Since I was born in Poland and I had been living for short time in Krakow, I could be a good guide for her. Then she added, "Rich, you have so much money, we could travel a lot." First Lady, just like her stepdaughter I.T., had super plans. I thought I.T. had good plans, but her stepmother M. absolutely beat her. In those few minutes, M.T. told me a lot about herself. We were talking a lot about her work. She knew everything about me and my work from TV and newspapers. She told me modeling is hard work and very stressful. She added it was not always models who are modeling in the nude. At that time, I had had one Remy Martin French Cognac and I was very cool and I hadn't been too shocked, just a little bit. I replied, "You are a very beautiful woman and you are not ashamed of your body. M… you have something to show. Millions of beautiful women, models are modeling in the nude every day." That's a model's job, after that discussion I thought to myself; she was a little bit nervous after that, she said to me. After all, we didn't know each other that well or for that long, but she still shared with me her secrets. But she knew that was maybe that was her only occasion to tell me all that.

I like M…very much and their whole family. They are great people. MT's husband DT is very generous person. Also I.T. has good hart, and decorating talent. I'm very impressed with the way she furnished and decorated my unit at the tower. I was grateful to her for the all clothes she bought for me, after her father asked her to do that. I mean, she bought everything from A–Z. Nothing was missing, not even a toothbrush or handkerchief. I.T., she has good eye, vision, and good taste.

After those few minutes of our conversation, MT and I split. She had her duties, and I had my duty. People are saying that MT is very shy. I didn't notice that with me. She was very open and a smooth talker. Once, about a year ago, I wrote to her and advised her that she should be more active and be seen more. Domestically and on an international arena. She took my advice, and now anytime President DT travels she is always with him. I like that, that's good for her and for our country. I like M very much. I'm always wishing her a lot of success and also for her whole family. After some time I walked to the bar and took my wallet out of my pocket. I pulled out one hundred dollars and I put it in the tip glass. I don't know who made me do that—it felt like my guardian angel was asking me to tip that much. Bartenders were shocked. One of them asked. "Who is this guy?" I ordered a Remy Martin from a frosted bottle and that's when the party really started to pick up.

BC and GB were standing next to me. BC asked me "Do you know what you've just done? Do you know how much that is?"

I said, "This is for the entire night"

Bill C said, "He is a trillionaire."

George B said, "Billionaire."

Bill C repeated, "Trillionaire." He asked me what I ordered.

I said, "Rémy Martin French cognac." They ordered the same thing and asked me if I would like to sit next to them and keep them company. My answer was yes. After some time sitting and talking with George B, Bill C, HRC, and LB. I was asked to go and make a speech.

I start the speech with, "Good evening," and I finished the speech with, "Bless the United States of America—the greatest country on Earth. Let's keep it this way." I also said many more things about American prosperity and wealth, and about the strength of our leaders, and about foreign policy. Everybody loved my speech. I received a long, standing ovation.

I got back to my table, and we sipped cognac and talked. HRC said, "Hey guys, what are you drinking?"

B said, "Rémy Martin, French cognac." She asked how it was, and B said, "Very good. Do you want to try it?" B was trying to give her his glass, but she said she would drink from my glass. Maybe she would have better luck. After all, many people thought I was lucky. Really, I was just blessed through the goodness of the Lord. But she still tried it from my glass. And after she tried it, she said it was good.

I asked if they wanted me to go order for them. HRC and LB said yes. I went to the bar and ordered for them, and I said to the bartender not to worry if we had a couple of extra glasses on the table.

After dinner, MK. came up to me and asked me to go with her. She took me to a private room, and we were talking about different things for a very long time. We talked about how I came to be such close friends and advisors with such powerful people. We talked about how I came to meet the Lord and about the healing miracles I performed. We also talked about the future of the country and how I would help lead America and keep it wealthy and prosperous and powerful. When we were finished talking, I went back to the table.

When I came back to our table, he said to me, "Rich, I was worried about you. I thought you would never come back. Then he said, "Before you left, you should have asked me about that secret room."

I said to him, "I have been there."

He asked me, "How did you know how to get there?"

I told them there was a sign, room. They were laughing. I said, "I'm just kidding; she took me there."

George B asked me, "How did she know about that room?"

I told him, "Maybe one time she was an intern here." They were laughing.

Next, George B said, "Rich, you have to drink a hundred dollars' worth of Cognac."

I said, "We already did."

He said, "No, you have to drink it yourself."

HRC said, "What?" George told her the story about the tip. She said, "Tip up in the front." I told them, "We like what we're doing to have a better service. Tip up in the front, because at the end it's too late, the damage is done."

George B said, "Never thought of it." He liked that idea.

Next, they asked me to go to a press conference. There was a large press conference happening with many reporters. One reporter was asking me many questions. She asked me, "Sir, you sometimes criticize people too much."

I thought to myself, I have to act quickly. I asked, "Did you watch the presidential campaign?"

She said, "I was in the campaign."

I asked, "Did you notice anything?"

She said, "What do you mean?"

I said, "Did you hear what they were saying?"

She said, "Every word."

I asked her, "What did they say?"

"Sir, I asked you a question."

I said, "We will get there." Then I slowly told her, "They were criticizing each other, right?"

She said, "Yes."

I asked her, "Is that good?"

She said, "Yes and no."

I said, "Wrong; it's good. When you see something, say something. Then negotiate and debate." I asked her, "Those steps are right, correct?" She said yes. I said, "No more questions. Next time, prepare yourself and do some more homework so that you don't waste people's time."

When I was walking away from the press conference and back to our table, another reporter said, "Sir, one quick question," which was similar to her question. I said to her just as I said before.

When I came to our table, George B asked me, "Rich, are you a lawyer or prosecutor?"

I said, "No, I'm a mechanic." I think that he was surprised to hear that. I think he expected me to be a lawyer or a prosecutor, based on my answers.

"Rich," George B said, "after that interview, some people are going to lose their jobs. I can only tell you that much." I think he wanted my advice, but he couldn't tell me too much.

Bill C seemed to want to change the conversation. He got up and said loudly, "Let's give him a standing ovation." I got a very long standing ovation; they didn't want to stop. Bill said to me, "Rich, you sit down. You did your job, now it's our job." Bill loudly said to the reporters while clapping his hands, "And don't even think to start with this man."

While walking on the dance floor with MT, I met and I had a very nice, long conversation with HRC. It was great to see her and to talk with her.

Later, I had been talking with the Cardinal and his mother. It was great to catch up with the Cardinal; I hadn't seen him for a while and missed speaking with him. We had a great conversation, and then she saw me speaking with him.

She asked me, "How do you know the Cardinal so well?"

I said, "Because I met with him a few times."

We continued to talk a little longer about the Cardinal, then about my life and about all of my money. Then she asked me, "Rich, what are you going to do with your money?"

I said, "I'm not worrying about that right now. Real estate is high, the stock market is too, so I'm waiting until it will go down."

George B overhead what I said about my money, and said, "So, you are spectacular."

I said, "No, I'm a businessman. You have to buy low and sell high. Otherwise, you will end up bankrupt."

A little later in the evening, while walking from the restroom, I was stopped. She is an anchorwoman at NBC news. I think she was happy to have an exclusive interview with me. She started with asking whom I was wearing that day. I said, "Canali."

"What kind of underwear? Boxers or briefs?"

"Briefs."

She asked me, "Why briefs?" and I said, "Because they are keeping everything in place. What kind of bra are you wearing? Loose or tight?"

She said, "Tight," and I said, "Why tight?"

She said, "To keep everything in place. What kind of watch are you wearing?" I showed it to her; she checked her phone and told me it's worth two and a half million dollars. It took one year to make, and it's the only one that was made. She added, "You have two and a half million dollars on your hand." I told her this didn't matter to me because I had more money than I could ever hope to spend in my entire lifetime. What was one watch?

She asked me if I'm staying in Washington or going back, and I said, "I'm going back."

"What time?

"When I am done here."

She said, "You don't have a ticket; you don't have a reservation on a plane. How are you going to get home?"

I said, "No, because I'm going to fly my helicopter." She asked me if I had a helicopter, and I said, "I have two."

She said, "Yellow and red?"

I asked her, "How did you know?" She told me it was because she interviewed me on the Roosevelt Aircraft Carrier off the Virginia coast on June 29, 2016. She wanted to party after we were done at the White House. I told her I would think about it.

When I got back to my table, George B said, "Rich, you are going to get married tonight." He said, "I can tell you that much." I wasn't sure why he said that, but I decided to play along.

I said, "Good. This will be a cheap wedding. Look, the Cardinal is sitting there. We had dinner, there was an open bar, we had dessert, and we have music."

George said, "Not so fast. We need another party." I realized he was serious, and that he really wanted to have another party for my wedding.

I said, "Once I settle down in New York City, I will throw a big party at the Waldorf Astoria."

HRC said, "Don't forget about them."

LB said, "And."

I said, "You are on the top of my list."

A little later that evening, I had been asked to go see the president. He wasn't too happy that I had been with them, but we had a nice conversation about the party and the evening. I told him I had met MT on the dance floor and I had a good conversation with her, and he seemed happy about that. After meeting with the president, I went to my table and spent some time talking with them again.

My guardian angel and partner for that night said, "Rich, we have to fly back."

I told them that I had a blast. I don't remember when I had such a great time, but George B said we have to get together more often. I agreed; I really enjoyed spending time with them and wanted to see more of them.

LB said, "George makes good steaks on the grill." She said that they would invite me to their place sometime soon for a barbeque. I agreed that would be nice, and that I would fly my helicopter to their place.

George B said, "Rich, thank you for introducing me to Rémy Martin. That's what I'm going to drink from now on. In Texas, I had been drinking tequila." He asked me, "Do you have anything on the helicopter? If not," he said, "I will go to the bar and get something for you."

I said, "There should be something."

Bill C said, "Sitting next to him, you will never fall asleep." He said, "When I first met him, I fell in love with this man." I was really grateful for my friendship with Bill and the others.

We walked to the front door. From there, Secret Service drove us to the airport, and my guardian angel and I flew back to Vernon, New Jersey.

Before I left, MK came up to me and asked me if I could drop her off in New York City. I said, "I don't know if we are allowed to take anyone." I knew that my guardian angel controlled who could fly on the helicopter, but I didn't have time to ask. I should have said yes, but it was too late.

At any meeting, I was a superstar. That party was no exception. I opened the party on the dance floor and received a standing ovation. Then I received standing ovations for my press conference and my speech. I also spoke with many powerful people at the White House who loved me.

Because I worked with the president and some of the other foreign leaders, I was supposed to work with the president as his advisor and live as his hotel in Washington, DC, during my time working with him. Everything was set—my clothes were already in closets there—but my higher authority stopped me from that job. I'm still not entirely sure why I was stopped, but I trusted my higher authority, so I went along with the decision. The Lord is always working in my favor.

At the meeting I had with the president, he asked me how old my partner, Little Angel, was. I replied, "Twenty-two."

He said, "Don't you think she is a little too young for you?" My answer was that she is just right. I wondered why he wasn't happy. I don't know why. Also, he was a little upset; he told me, "I was supposed to be in Washington on January 18, 2017, through January 20, 2017, but I arrived on January 20, 2017, late in the afternoon." The organizers were very nervous because I wasn't there and I had big roles to play. I was part pf that huge program that night. I had first started the party with dancing, then made a speech, then had an interview with the press and a certain guest. I did that and a lot more in that short time. Can you imagine if I would have been there since?

After I left, Bill C was talking with the president and told him for the first time in his whole life he met someone who could party. He wasn't wasting any time, and by the end of January 2017, he gave me a call with huge plans, a party on a mega-yacht.

I.T told me after I left the White House on Inauguration night that she was talking to her father and told him that she wants Rich. Her father replied, "He is a playboy."

She replied, "Good, good, that's why I want him." She is sweet! But he wasn't too happy because he would be very happy seeing me married to that one who got on her knee with that huge diamond ring. Who was she? She was a powerful news anchor. So what? The president and advisor Richard Langner and his new wife, a powerful news anchor, is always good news, for the president always thinks ahead. That does not always work well for him. Many times, he doesn't take good advice.

At the end of January, I.T. called me and told me that we were going to fly to Moscow to meet with President. She said that each time her father was talking to President, and he asked how Rich was doing. I thought it was wonderful that President remembered me. I figured I would have to take him up on his offer to fly to Moscow sometime soon.

February 15, 2017

On February 15, 2017, I.T did inspect all kitchen cabinets.

On February 15, 2017 I.T. did like and want all of that China

A few weeks later, on February 15, 2017, I met with at her condominium, not through the door or window either. She asked me how I got there. We spent some time discussing business; her and I both have great heads for money, business, and the economy. After we spent a couple of hours together, she called her father at the White House and told him that I, Richard Langner, was with her and offered her good business.

"Rich told me that he is going to rebrand my stuff and it's going to be put on Angel's retailers." She said to her father that Angel's retailers are the biggest retailers in the world. She added, "Rich said he will make double, triple, and even in some cases quadruple."

Many stores boycott her products. She needed help, and I was the only one who could help her. That was the first good news, but she had one more piece of information. She said to her father, "Dad, you are going to have a grandson."

Her father said, "What? What? When? How do you know?"

"Rich told me that." I was standing next to her, and her phone was on speaker, so I could hear every word.

After that, her father said, "We are going to do a big wedding in the United States.." Her father really loves her.

She replied, "No, Dad, forget it. I'm going to have a small wedding in Prague or Krakow. I want to have a normal life." I also asked her what name she was going to have, and she said she likes my name and she is going to have her name as Langner. I changed her first name by mistake, but she loves it. After the election, I wrote a letter to about how I changed her name by mistake.

After that, her father told her to go to his unit to get champagne and celebrate, and we did. There were a few bottles of Don Perignon champagne, which we took, drank, and celebrated with.

I was really shocked and didn't know about her plans. I asked, "When did you get that idea? You really planned that well."

"Yes, I did." She really went way in front of herself. I like her very much, she has it all, she's smart, she's talented, and she has the look. I mean, she's the full package. I would marry her if I only could. She's not the only one who wanted to marry me. You'd really be shocked if I were to make a list with only super famous women.

After she brought that champagne, I took that bottle in my hands, first with my left hand to warm up the bottle neck, and then I opened without any spilling.

She said, "How did you do that without spilling?" I told her how I did it and she really liked that. While celebrating, we were talking about everything, especially after a few glasses of champagne. IT is a very intelligent young woman, so it's easy to communicate with her. She said that she wants to get married in one month.

I said, "That soon?"

On February 15, 2017, I and Yvona T. were standing in the front of this window.

She said in this situation that's the best way to do it. I was angry. At one point she asked me if I was hungry, but before I was able to answer she said, "Your clothes are here; take a shower, dress yourself, and let's go to a restaurant to eat." She's the one who bought all the clothes for me after her father told her to do that on January 9, 2017, when we had the meeting at before the inauguration. Someone coordinated the whole thing. She was at my unit because my clothes were there. She was surprised when she saw me, but she had been very happy seeing me. Instead of going to the restaurant, we found ourselves in my condominium in Vernon, NJ.

We didn't know how we got to my condominium in Vernon. We were standing next to each other and she asked me, "How did we get here?"

I said, "I don't know." Once we got inside my condo, for a few minutes she started looking around, pulling out drawers and opening cabinets. She loved all the china. While in the kitchen, she asked what I was cooking. I replied, "Almost everything—breaded chicken cutlets, fish fillets, pork chops." First, I beat the eggs, made dip, fish, and meat, and then put in breadcrumbs. I gave her a couple more recipes. For beef rollups, I cut ten slices of beef, rounded and tender, and next I apply a thin layer of mustard. Then a slice of green pepper and ten long slices of pickle, then I roll them up and keep them close. I use toothpicks, and also you could use white thread. Next, I said, "Potato Pancakes."

"Please give me the recipe, I don't want to wait for you to make them."

"I will make them right away, then." I did give her that recipe. Next, we went to the bedroom. When we were in my bedroom, she saw pictures hanging on the wall taken in the Botanical Gardens in the Bronx, NY. She asked me where they were taken, and I told her the Botanical Gardens. She said she's never been there, and I told her that my family and I go there a few times a year.

She replied, "You live in New Jersey and you're going there. I'm living in New York City, which is so close and yet I've never been there. When we were young, our father always said, 'study, study, study.' Now it's 'work, work, work.' We didn't go anywhere." She opened the closet and asked me if I ironed my shirts. I said yes, and sleeves without crease.

She asked me if I would iron for her. I said no; she asked again, saying, "But if I said, 'Rich, I'm running late and I want to wear this blouse,' could you please do this for me?" I said yes. She was happy. Then she pulled out a drawer with bathing suits and said, "You have more than I do. Why?" She also asked me if I could cook for us. I said sometimes. See for yourself, she is smart and made sure her near-future husband was good. She was happy.

At one moment Yvona and I went to the window and looked out at the pond and mountains. On the right side of my window there grew a tall cedar tree, about fifty feet. In 2013 I planted two chestnut seeds next to that tree and in 2014 they popped out. Ever since it's grown to about six! One manager of this resort asked me if they could replant it in a different spot by professionals. I said, "No, I don't want this chestnut to die." I showed that chestnut to IT, and she very quickly asked if I could dig one out. I said no because it could die. She replied that would be done by a professional. She was so sweet and asked the same thing, why I couldn't say no. I said, "That smaller one you could dig out." When I talked with the Lord at the end of spring, he wasn't happy about my decision, but I reminded Him that once we were talking about that, they were tied. After that, he was okay.

The inspection wasn't done yet. She went to my desk, and when she pulled the drawer from my desk, she took my "Porsche Design" sunglasses and said she could wear them. Then invisible said, "They're mine," but I gave them to the little angel. Then she took the box with my pinky finger ring, which was horseshoe-shaped with diamonds.

She said, "I could wear it."

Invisible said, "Gabriela's."

After that she asked me, "Who is that?"

I said, "That's Little Angel, the one with whom I have been at the White House with on Inauguration Day. Ramona and Gabriela's mother." I asked her to write to the Cardinal to share her experiences with him. I figured the Cardinal would want to hear from other people about the miracles I performed, like bringing IT and myself all the way to my condominium. I wanted the Cardinal to keep those records all together or to pass them to the Vatican and keep them at the Vatican museum for future generations. This is one of the reasons I'm writing this. I know the Church is investigating this whole thing. My miracle is easy to prove. It is on camera, the Cardinal witnessed himself. The Pope witnessed himself. I delivered him the letter from New Jersey to Vatican. I didn't fly on an airplane Also I didn't get to the Vatican by ship either. I had dinner at a restaurant in Hamburg, NJ, with my family. All of the family I saw at that restaurant had already been dead; they died a long time ago, but Cardinal Dolan has a copy of a film from the restaurant camera of that day.

He told me at the White House, "That's your family on that film." The miracle at the hospital and on and on. That's why I asked to add one more miracle to the Cardinal's collection. I believe these miracles are sent to remind people about God, and to behave themselves. The end is up to one person, and it could happen sooner than anyone can imagine. The Cardinal knows that. I don't think he wants this to happen. That's why he doesn't want me to do what I asked him to do. But I don't need anyone.

After, I was shown many places in Vernon, like the wine cellar at Crystal Spring Golf and Spa. It is a world-class cellar with one hundred thousand to two hundred thousand bottles of wine. Then I showed her my shop. She said, "I want it and all that is in. I want to make a museum." How can you not like that kind of person? After that, I sent her home by herself the same way we together came to New Jersey, in no time.

A few months after my visit to Vatican City, on March 9, 2017, I had a visitor named Mike, a police officer, whose father I previously healed from lung cancer. Mike brought his police chief with him because the chief's wife had cancer all over her body. They also lived in my town, Vernon, NJ. Her husband asked me if I could help her. I said to him, "I will do my best." I truly wanted to heal this woman. I traveled with Mike and the police chief to the chief's house.

After we got to his house and met with her, I touched her body and I said to her, "Get back to your good health and be healthy again." She seemed to brighten immediately; I saw the color return to her pale face. I saw her eyes lighten up. I think she knew that the Lord had sent me to perform a miracle. After that, her health started to improve. I never heard from the police chief or his wife again, but Mike told me that the wife, eventually, healed completely.

These are only some of my experiences. All witnesses are alive, so it is easy to verify those miracles.

Not all of my miracles are based in actions; I know things too. For example, the end of the world could be sooner than anyone thinks. Ask the Cardinal from New York City. He heard that from me, and also from my angel and negotiator. He and I both heard how and when the world will end. My negotiator told the Cardinal to not do what I had asked him to do because after that would be the end of the world. But I don't need any help. After that, the world would be much better.

On CNN, they said that the end of the world is coming. Someone from my circle told him that. My guardian angel told me that I'm going to judge he living and the dead. Like you see, a lot of things have happened since I wrote the last letter. The Lord's car is parked where I'm living; it's under the apple tree and it has been there for many months.

Also, I would like you to know that for those medals I received in June of 2016 on the Roosevelt Aircraft Carrier from the president; my negotiator asked me what I wanted to do with those medals—keep them or send them to the museum? I told him to take them to the museum. I believe they are at the Vatican museum. You are welcome to visit them, and to inform others about the medals now that you are aware of them.

On February 15, 2017, Yvona T checked out every drawer in this dresser.

Yvonna T checked every drawer at my desk

January 19, 2019

Me and my wife we drove on route 517 S. Once we passed great Gorge South Ski Resort, which was located on route 94 and 517 South, we made a left turn on Route 517 South. After we drove less than one quarter of a mile up the hill, we saw the Lord standing on the hiking trail and Route 517 S. On his back he had a backpack. It was noon.

He meant I should just ask the "Higher Authority" for him to always be around me. The Lord loves those mountains and hiking there.

Also, that night, Jesus Christ asked me this way, "You wouldn't mind if I would take a shower in your bathroom?"

I replied, "Please take a shower." I did not see or hear him taking a shower. They can be visible and in a second, they can be invisible. Who wouldn't do anything for our Lord?

January 24, 2019

I met the Lord at Newton, New Jersey, at a ShopRite supermarket. I was talking with him for a while. Then he waited for me outside and we were talking some more. We were talking about everything. He was always around me; sometimes he wanted to talk. He was dressed nicely in the Coast Guard tactical uniform with a matching hat. That uniform had brown, green spots and dark beige, the typical tactical uniform.

May 3, 2019

I was passing the ski area and saw the Lord walking on the ski slope at Great Gorge South by the lodge right at the bottom. It was very muddy, the snow was melting, and days before, we had rain. Like always, in his right hand he was holding his walking stick. "That's his logo"; on his back he was carrying a backpack. That's our Lord. No one else would even think to go on the slopes in that kind of condition. But he knew I was heading in that direction, and he wanted me to see him. He can't show himself, only if there is a reason.

January 10, 2020

On January 10, 2020, I was watching the History Channel and the program was Ancient Aliens. There were two perfect guys in black. Those two guys could do impossible things. When I had been at Great Gorge on January 13, 2016, those two guys who came up to me at the Great Gorge South and they looked exactly like these characters. When I initially saw them, I was shocked, but now I have a much clearer picture of who they are.

Some people one time saw a UFO and called the police, and then the police called the Air Force. From the Air Force they sent three F-16s to chase them there. When those F-16s got close to the UFO aircraft, from the UFO aircraft they start shooting at those F-16s, something like fire balls of light, to prevent them from taking pictures and shooting them down. What happened there was that in that area there was a cruise ship, so people were taking perfect pictures of that situation. People from the "UFO" knew about that cruise ship, so they sent these two guys in black to go meet with the captain and demand all those films from the cameras. They had so much power that the captain couldn't resist. He just did what they asked. Somehow, someone kept one because people found out on the news.

Now I'm the one who has the last word and the power. Nothing comes easily; you must set your own goals and go for it. In this country all doors are open to everyone, but you must work hard. Today and the whole Martin Luther King Day I had been writing stories. I was supposed to be skiing in Pennsylvania with my wife and daughters and grandson, who is seven and a half years old. I chose instead to compile this book and have my true untold story and incredible miracles with 100 percent proof.

Four years ago, I had a press conference at Red Tail Lodge. That was on January 17, 2016, over Martin Luther King weekend. That weekend and also four years later I'm writing what happened then and until now through 2020.

June 1, 2020

On the president's Inauguration Day on January 20, 2017, when I had a meeting with the president, the president said to me, "You are so famous, you won't be able to get anything done."

That night I was so busy; there had been heavy traffic around me. He didn't like that too much, because he was supposed to be the one with all the attention.

On March 13, 2019, I wrote a letter to the president. I reminded him what he said to me at the Oval Office on January 20, 2017. I wrote to him: What you said was wrong, incorrect. Only famous people, people with knowledge can achieve their goals. If you want to be reelected, something very good must happen or another miracle.

After he received my letter on March 16, 2019, he lost his mind. The whole weekend he was texting, blaming John McCain for not voting to repeal Obamacare. John McCain was supposed to vote for repeal, but when he came from Arizona to Washington, DC, at the last minute he changed his mind and voted against repeal.

The president, after that, on September 22, 2017, was furious; he was mad at John McCain, and he still is. He was so furious he even said that was an act of God. Maybe he was right.

You cannot replace something with nothing. He still doesn't have a better plan. Media anchors and others were losing their minds. They didn't know what was wrong with DT. Only I know what happened to him.

For the president to repeal Obamacare was that very good thing, and he lost that. And that could cost him reelection, which was very painful.

On June 28, 2019, I received a letter from the president. He wrote:

Thank you for taking the time to write to me. Your kind words and steadfast support mean a great deal. Every day, I am working to uphold the values we cherish and to better serve the American people. My administration is focused on promoting freedom and opportunity so that our nation continues to thrive. As a result, a renewed sense of optimism is spreading through cities and towns across our nation. Thank you again for your support. I am confident that together we will continue to build a stronger and more prosperous nation for all Americans.

In the beginning of 2020, we got bad news: a new unknown, terrible disease started spreading around the world. Also, it started spreading across our country. The president and his administration thought that this disease would miraculously vanish, disappear.

Each time the president is in trouble he thinks the miracle will happen and will resolve his problems. We elected the president to resolve all our problems. But he was still waiting for that miracle. He knew if that miracle would happen, his reelection would be a guarantee.

I saw the president and his administration hesitating and they didn't know what to do. I decided to write a letter to the president at the end of May 2020:

Dear Mr. President,

The whole world and our great nation are in terrible turmoil. Our country is leading the world in both cases and deaths. We knew that a timely decision was very important in every case. In this case, it mattered that we lost that time under pressure; we lost about two months. That's a lot, and now we are paying the heavy price.

June 1, 2020, the biggest chaos in Washington D.C.

After the president received the letter from me, they still were waiting for a miracle. When they were on national television, she was talking about dying children. She sounded like she was waiting, asking for a miracle. I know the president prepared that speech for. The president's attorney said that is talking in codes and also acting in codes. You need to know him to understand him when he is acting and talking in codes. But first you will need to know the subject.

In this letter, I reminded the president what I wrote to him in the letter from March 2019. I wrote in it that if you want to be reelected, something very good must happen or another miracle. Is that going to happen again?

Since March 13, 2019, my friend, nothing very good happened. Only one disaster after another. So, like you see, we can count only on another miracle. Is that going to happen? We will see. In 2016 we were all working together very hard to win that election and we succeeded. This time, the second round doesn't look too good. Our economy is down, our debt is the highest in our history, unemployment is the highest ever, chaos in our streets across the country. In this situation, it will be very hard to win in this coming election.

After the president received the letter from me on June 1, 2020, right away he organized a march from the White House to St. John Episcopal Church in Lafayette Square in Washington, DC. President, AG, IT, JK, and others were present in that march. MT wasn't marching with them. What was the reason for them to march to the Church in the biggest chaos in Washington, DC?

The president was walking with the Bible in his hand up in front, and the rest followed him. But first they used a helicopter and gas to clear that passage from the White House to St. John Episcopal Church, because that demonstration was really dangerous. Once the president got in front of St. John Episcopal Church, he lifted the Bible up above his head and moved it a few times. He reminded me of a priest with a Bible on the Church altar. Without a word said, President DT then turned around and walked back to the White House.

What was the reason for that? They said they went for a photo session. President A.G. and others simply went there to ask God for help for a miracle, another miracle. That was a code act. No one knew why they really went.

The president was walking with the Bible in his hand toward the St. John Episcopal Church, once he got in front of it, he lifted the Bible above his head, then moved it few times. After that he turned around and walked back to the White House.

In the biggest chaos in Washington D.C. D.J.T., I.T, J., K., A.G. and others march to St. John Episcopal Church.

Therefore, just like the president said a few times on national television that he must ask God if this is the proper time to reopen businesses, because this will be his most important decision he will ever make in his whole life.

House judiciary committee hearing of attorney general WB on July 28, 2020, in Washington, DC. Senator CC asked BB, "When did you find out that you are going to walk to St. John Episcopal Church in Lafayette Square in Washington, DC, with President IK, the general, and others? In the time of the worse chaos in Washington, DC, when they used helicopter, gas, police, and agents to clear a path from the White House to St. John Episcopal Church. Bill B replied," I found out about that on June 1, 2020, late afternoon." That was after president D. J. T. received letter from me.

On August 31, 2020, LI interviewed DJT. She was asking him who was running JB's campaign, the former President O? He replied, "No, people who are walking on the streets wearing black suits, shadowing people." LI didn't know what he was talking about, she was shocked. Also, all the anchors who are running news shows on CNN, NBC, FOX, and other stations. Also, he said full airplane of "thugs," people in black suits.

President J. did experience miracles, and he wants more each time he's in trouble or when he wants to make something impossible happen. His daughter experienced many miracles, most of them which happened on February 15, 2017. First at my condominium at T Tower, 721 5th Ave. in New York City, and then between New York City and Vernon, NJ, and more in Vernon, New Jersey.

That's why J. is always asking and looking for miracles. Because, with miracles, things are done quickly and easily. If he wants to be successful and achieve his goals, he must use his head and work hard. That's the only way— the best way.

When interviewed on August 31, 2020, she asked him, "Who is running Joe's campaign? The former President?"

He replied, "No, shady people, people who are walking on the street in, people in black suits."

Laura I. didn't know what he was talking about. She was shocked. Also anchors who were running shows on CNN, NBC, Fox News. Once again was talking in codes. I assume he was talking about people in black suits and tall hats, who came from above to help Joe. Did know them? If he knew them, does he have any proof?

On July 28, 2020, in Washington, DC, Bill was asked by a senator, "When did you find out about walking to St. John Episcopal Church with the president and others?"

That was in the middle of the worst chaos in Washington. He replied, "I found out about this on June 1, 2020, late afternoon." That afternoon, the president received a letter from me.

People in black suits were heading to Washington, DC, to RNC to interrupt the convention. The president said those "thugs" in black suits were now investigated by the FBI. Are those people in black suits are the same or similar to those who I met at "Hink Bourbon Bar" at "Great Gorge South," now "Mountaincreek Resort," on February 13, 2016?

Once again, the president talked in codes. He didn't know what he was talking about. I assume he was talking about people who came from somewhere just to help to win the presidential election. Does know them? Has he met them? Has he any proof that they exist?

October 8, 2020
Pisces Horoscope - Astrology...
Like a butterfly emerging from its chrysalis, you've taken some pretty tough circumstances and used them to grow. Now you are developing into something lovely and fantastic beyond your wildest imaginings. During times like these it's good to remember how grateful you are, not only for easy things in your life but also for the tough circumstances. They have shaped you into someone amazing. Take a moment to honor yourself.

Sometimes I receive information from my guardian angels—advisors—through my horoscope sign.

On October 8, 2020, they wrote this.

October 21, 2020
I would like to add and explain a few things. When I have been talking with the Lord, on March 17, 2015, the Lord asked me why I don't have long hair. I replied because I have thin hair in front and a lot in the back of my head.

He replied, "Pull them out," and added "If you want to be in Heaven, you need to have long hair."

On January 17, 2016, at Red Tail Lodge, my negotiator told me that I don't need long hair because "I don't like long hair." Also, that night the Lord said to me, "Do you think that's a coincidence that we look alike?" After that night talk, I had with the Lord, I knew he was my friend.

I asked him if he liked me; he replied, "No, I don't." I asked him why, and he said, "You have too much power over me." The Lord is 180 degrees different than what he once was. Being jealous is a sin.

Another thing, on October 26, 2016, when I hosted a press conference with presidential candidates, and announced, "I gave a condominium at to Richard

Langner." He added that his daughter was decorating the condominium for him. Also, she bought clothes for me, after her father told her to do so. He told me what to do, to get the key to my unit. I followed his instructions, and when I got to the tower, that man who made the phone call to somewhere said to me, "There is nothing in your name." The Cardinal was at that press conference and many others. My family saw that press conference on TV news.

I would like to inform you what they could do. For example, there could be a full room of people, but they can make me invisible inside that room and also to that person they want me to see and talk to. That person would give me wrong information, the information they want me to get. I assume that's what happened on the day I went to T Tower to get the key to my condominium.

I experienced this with when we were moving from place to place, and no one could see us or hear us talking.

I have another example. On February 15, 2017, at my condominium during my conversation with her, I was made mute—disconnected for some time, and during that period of time, someone invisible said to her, "We will rebrand your product and we will put that on 'Angel Retailers,' and you will make double, triple, and even quadruple for your products."

I didn't hear that conversation. I found out later about that, when I.T. called her father to the White House and told him that Rich Langner offered her good business. He said that he was going to rebrand my products and he was going to put it on "Angel Retailers," and I was going to make double, triple, and even quadruple for my products.

After that, her father said to her to go to my unit, and there were a few bottles of Don Perignon champagne to celebrate, and we did.

The same thing happened at St. Patrick's Cathedral in New York City at the end of June 2016, when they married me to my guardian angel, "Little Angel." I gave her that name because they don't have names. When I got in front of the Cardinal, he said that it would be a short ceremony because I was running late and I was flying to meet with the president on the Roosevelt Aircraft Carrier on the Virginia coast.

After that, they made me unconscious. I was disconnected. I didn't know what was going on. I regained my conscious after the ceremony. I assume the Cardinal didn't notice anything unusual. After the ceremony I had a short conversation with the Cardinal. After I stopped talking with the Cardinal, once again, I lost consciousness—memory. Once again, I regained my conscious when I got on my yellow helicopter.

Most of those who come here from above on special mission are not saints. Saints are in Heaven. There are some exceptions like the ones I prayed with: St. Pope John Paul II, at St. Francis De Sales Church in Vernon, New Jersey, on February 8, 2015...

From my guardian advisors, this time they advised me to make the right decision and said loudly what I (you) know.

Pisces Horoscope Astrology. December 23, 2020 Sometime soon, you'll need to make a decision whether or not to let a secret see the light of day. That's not an easy thing for you because you can usually see both sides of the issue. Use that famous intuition of yours to make that decision and above all else, don't repeat. Do not feel guilty if your ultimate choice is to let the truth be told. Clearing the air is always the best tactic, if not immediately, then in the long run.

Since February 2005 me and my wife have been living on golf course by the pond and fourth hole. Our condominium is set that way so when the bad golfers and beginners are playing, their golf balls are landing in front of our windows, since our window is only forty feet away from the fourth hole. In the first seven years of our living in this unit, our windows were never broken. Then in nine years, three times. A year ago one of our windows started getting foggy. To replace that window would have cost about three hundred dollars. Was still not too bad. So, we didn't rush to replacement. An about May 12, 2021, my wife said to me, when we were talking about replacement because the windows were getting really bad, she said to me maybe some bad golfer is going to hit the window with the golf ball and break it. She was just kidding. When a golfer broke window, the association replaced it without charging owners. On Sunday May 16, 2021, we went to Church, ten o'clock Mass, and after the Mass we drove to Warwick, New York, a nice, small town, with so many good restaurants with great food. That day we went there for lunch. After the lunch we went to the farmer's market. There is always plenty of fresh stuff. We didn't really rush; the weather that day very nice and sunny. We like stay outside for as long as possible. When we got home, we noticed that the foggy window was hit by a golf ball and was broken. Just four days after my wife's wish. Her wish had been fulfilled. On Monday I went to the association office to report the damage and that incident which happened on Sunday. The lady who was working at the association office informed me that someone would come to our condominium to check it and take the measurements a couple days later. A person from the glass company came, took all necessary measurements, and he informed us that in about two weeks he would be able to replace this broken window. We were very happy. On Sunday May 23, 2021, we did what we had done the previous Sunday. We went to Church for the ten o'clock Mass, then after the Mass we drove to Warwick for lunch, and after that, on way home we stopped at Shop Rite to pick up some groceries.

When we got home, we found out that another golf ball went through the hole the first golf ball made in that foggy window on the previous Sunday, on May 16, 2021. Every window has two glass plates and in between its gas.. The second ball doesn't touch the first glass in the windows, went perfectly through that small hole in the window and broke the second glass plate. Now we were in big trouble, We vacuumed all the glass off the floor, next I took plastic bag (white) and covered that hole, I taped with scotch tape to prevent rainwater to get inside home. On Monday, once again I went to the association office to report what happened the previous day. That lady who was working there that day had been laughing after she heard the story I told her with the second golf ball, which went through the hole the first golf ball made in the window. Once again the glass guy came up, and this time he secured that second window with plywood. Two weeks later he came back and replaced broken window. My wife's wish came true; that wasn't a coincidence. That was proved with the second golf ball that second golf ball went exactly in the same spot. Perfect shot after the first ball hit that window, after my wife wished for it, I knew someone want to send some signal to proof something. After the second golf ball went through the hold the first ball made, that was proof that someone was directing it. That was not a coincidence on the nights of May 31 to June 1, 2021. I had been wake up by some noise; people were talking in my bedroom, there was some crying, but I couldn't understand anything. It lasted maybe for one or two minutes, then was quiet for about few seconds; after that short break of silence my negotiator started talking to me. I didn't see anybody. He said to me the man with all the power drove those golf balls into that window. I knew that would be much easier to hit the mega bowl than from that far hit the window in the same spot with two golf balls. Even the best snipers with the long gun won't be able to shoot two bullets into exactly the same spot. Miracles are only to prove something, just like healing someone, it's not we want to heal someone, just to prove something, signal something, point, show the power, warning someone. It was warning all the people on this earth. God is watching people on the earth and he it is getting upset at what he is seeing. I had been talking with my negotiator about the end of the world. They don't want that, Saint Mary doesn't want that either. Just like she said in Fatima, Portugal, in 1917 five times between April 13 and October 13, 1917. She said God is getting mad; she asked people to get better. Instead, people are getting worse and worse. It's a crime; it's very high.

I've written this already in the beginning of my book that the Lord came here with army of angels to protect me and prepare me for something big. Just like he yelled at the press conference at the R.T. lodge when I entered the room where press conference was set. "Stop the music! Here comes the King, the New King.: So they came here to prepare me to be the New King. I'm asking myself, What is the Lord's role today? I don't know why I never asked him, maybe because he doesn't want me to ask him that. We all know that he is supposed to sit at the right hand of the father; instead, he came here and he likes to be here. What's really shocking me is that Pope F. never responded to me after I sent him a ton of information. Pope F. never wrote to me, or asked any questions; he knows, and he has all proof from Vernon Pastor and the Cardinal of New York. Cardinal D. shared with Pope all he knew. Also, I did visit Pope F. in Vatican. I did travel to Vatican not by train, airplane, or by ship. I just got there somehow. I do have my old passport and new too. I had never been to Italy before that visit to Vatican. And in the way normally people travel.

I've written this already in the beginning of my book that the Lord came here with army of angels to protect me and prepare me for something big. Just like he yelled at the press conference at the R.T. lodge when I entered the room where press conference was set. "Stop the music! Here comes the King, the New King.: So they came here to prepare me to be the New King. I'm asking myself, What is the Lord's role today? I don't know why I never asked him, maybe because he doesn't want me to ask him that. We all know that he is supposed to sit at the right hand of the father; instead, he came here and he likes to be here. What's really shocking me is that Pope F. never responded to me after I sent him a ton of information. Pope F. never wrote to me, or asked any questions; he knows, and he has all proof from Vernon Pastor and the Cardinal of New York. Cardinal D. shared with Pope all he knew. Also, I did visit Pope F. in Vatican. I did travel to Vatican not by train, airplane, or by ship. I just got there somehow. I do have my old passport and new too. I had never been to Italy before that visit to Vatican. And in the way normally people travel. Why? After the Cardinal of New York had all the proof from Vernon, NJ, Church, Hamburg restaurant, he married me with a guardian angel, at St. Patrick's Cathedral of New York, admitted to me at the White House on Inauguration Day in January 20, 2017 that those people in the Hamburg restaurant were my family. Also that person who was holding my hand while prayed at St. Francis de Sale Church in Vernon, NJ, had been St. Pope John Paul II. Still, no one contacted me to ask me some questions and ask me to show them all those places where I met the Lord. I sent pictures of the Lord's car, parked on M. Resort parking lot and still is today, is November 14, 2021, and that Toyota Prius, it is still park there, since January 2021. Once they wanted to tow away that car, but I put a note on the windshield and asked them to leave that car alone because that's the Lord's car. Ever since I left that note on the windshield, no one bothers his car anymore. On December 24, 2021, the Lord's car was moved and ever since, it's been parked under the same apple tree like the previous one. I'm waiting for the right time to organize a press conference by that car. I sent letter with a picture to the Pope and Cardinal D. I did that twice, still no response. I believe high priests like to keep things they are for centuries. I'm shocked. The Lord was called back and he left the earth. On May 31 to June 1, 2021, I was talking at midnight with Lord's and my negotiator; he told me that the Lord, when back, would like to come back home. The Lord and the others want me to call him back here. I need to find out what the stories are. When I was talking with my negotiator, I asked him, "What's going on with my condo at T. Tower in New York City?" He replied, "We are holding the deed because we want a piece of that condominium." Even after was given to me as a gift and it's in my name. M.T., at the White House, said to me, "Rich, that condo is in your name." They are afraid only of one thing: if I will move out from here, they will need to go back. They don't want to go where they came from; they are doing all kind of manipulations just to stay here. Just like she said to me, my number-one guardian angel at my office on November 12, 2012, "We came here to destroy you because you won't work with us." They still doing the same thing, but it's not easy to win with me and they know that. We have law here on earth; they don't want to respect that, but I will made them to respect because I'm the one with all the power and they know that.

I want to go back to our Pope F. after I send to him my early manuscript with all those pictures, drawings, and maps. I still didn't receive from him letter with any questions. Maybe I did the perfect job. I sent all proofs and explained everything clearly to him and maybe there'snothing left to ask for. I believe there is always something left to ask, and find out something untold.

I would like to share my true, untold experiences with people of the world.

On November 12, 2012, while eating lunch at my office, I was looking through the window facing Route 23 when I turned my head to the left. I noticed a woman was standing about three feet away from me and I said to her, "How did you get here? The door is locked."

She said, "It's locked; go check." I didn't move. She repeated, "It's locked; go check." I didn't move again; I was afraid of getting up and leaving the room. Strangely enough, I didn't want this woman to leave—even though I had no idea who she was or where she had come from. She noticed my hesitation. Again, she said, "Go, go, go." I got up and I checked, and the door was locked.

That day was very cold, but this woman was wearing a white dress with short sleeves. She had no shoes on her feet and her face was foggy; I couldn't see it clearly. I asked her, "Are you not cold?" She said she didn't have blood. I said, "I have a clean fleece jacket and I can give it to you." She said, "I do not need your jacket; I am not cold."

Then she asked me, "You don't want to live anymore?" I wondered at how she knew that, but I decided to answer her. Something about her seemed ethereal.

I said, "I lost a lot of money on the stock market. The auto business is finished. I have been buying new or couple-years-old total loss cars at auto insurance auctions. After I rebuild them, I sell those cars on eBay. That was great business—what I had been doing for thirty years. Computers destroyed this kind of business. People from all around the world were betting on computers, and we couldn't compete with Africa, South America, China, and Eastern Europe."

She said, "We came here to destroy you because you won't work with us, but we misjudged you. You will get a big house and lots of money." I was startled at that; I still had no idea who this woman was, or where she had come from, or why she had come to destroy me. But I was curious about her prediction.

I asked her, "When?" She said, "Very soon." Then she said, "I have to go." I asked her to stay but she said she must go then. I asked her if she could come back tomorrow, and she told me that one day she will be back.

They were destroying me and my family in every possible way. She, specifically, damaged my car, broke windows in our garage and the door locks after I said I was going to sell my garage to my son for one dollar.

The Lord said something was wrong. I don't want to write that word. He is not who you think he is. Why were they doing that? Because they were living there in my garage. That was their home, which they were protecting every possible way. They came here in 2002. Then my guardian angel said, "We misjudged you. You will get back what you lost."

When we were talking, she told me, "Look for the house and they will pay for it." I had been on the Trulia website looking for houses in Sparta, NJ, and my guardian angel must have known that. She made it sound like all would be well, once I found the house I wanted to buy—like someone else would purchase the house. So, I kept going.

November 12, 2012

I was very confused about what had happened. It felt like an angel had visited me. But because I did not understand who she was or what had happened, I continued to live my life as usual. At that time, my shop was on the market for sale, but this woman came to me again and told me I couldn't sell the garage because that was her home. When she left, she went up with a loud sound. She was also the mother of our daughter, Sophia, who was, at this time, two years old. Now, eight years later, she is close to ten years old.

In November 2012 I had been at the farmer's market. She had nothing in her hands, but she came very close to me, still smiling, and stood in front of me for a few seconds, turned around, and she went outside. That was in November of 2012. Later, I found out from the leader of guardian angels that she was the number two guardian angel. The Lord came here with army of angels to do a special job. I assume to prepare me for something big. An average person won't get this. It's easy for me to talk with Cardinal D because he met with my organizer many times, who is from above, in heaven, and that there was competition for the number-one spot.

April 4, 2013

In Aruba, I was walking on the beach and noticed a young Black woman walking toward me. She was wearing long slacks and a long burgundy wool winter coat over them. She was chic and lovel

I've written this already in the beginning of my book that the Lord came here with army of angels to protect me and prepare me for something big. Just like he yelled at the press conference at the R.T. lodge when I entered the room where press conference was set. "Stop the music! Here comes the King, the New King.: So they came here to prepare me to be the New King. I'm asking myself, What is the Lord's role today? I don't know why I never asked him, maybe because he doesn't want me to ask him that. We all know that he is supposed to sit at the right hand of the father; instead, he came here and he likes to be here. What's really shocking me is that Pope F. never responded to me after I sent him a ton of information. Pope F. never wrote to me, or asked any questions; he knows, and he has all proof from Vernon Pastor and the Cardinal of New York. Cardinal D. shared with Pope all he knew. Also, I did visit Pope F. in Vatican. I did travel to Vatican not by train, airplane, or by ship. I just got there somehow. I do have my old passport and new too. I had never been to Italy before that visit to Vatican. And in the way normally people travel. Why? After the Cardinal of New York had all the proof from Vernon, NJ, Church, Hamburg restaurant, he married me with a guardian angel, at St. Patrick's Cathedral of New York, admitted to me at the White House on Inauguration Day in January 20, 2017 that those people in the Hamburg restaurant were my family. Also that person who was holding my hand while prayed at St. Francis de Sale Church in Vernon, NJ, had been St. Pope John Paul II. Still, no one contacted me to ask me some questions and ask me to show them all those places where I met the Lord. I sent pictures of the Lord's car, parked on M. Resort parking lot and still is today, is November 14, 2021, and that Toyota Prius, it is still park there, since January 2021. Once they wanted to tow away that car, but I put a note on the windshield and asked them to leave that car alone because that's the Lord's car. Ever since I left that note on the windshield, no one bothers his car anymore. On December 24, 2021, the Lord's car was moved and ever since, it's been parked under the same apple tree like the previous one. I'm waiting for the right time to organize a press conference by that car. I sent letter with a picture to the Pope and Cardinal D. I did that twice, still no response. I believe high priests like to keep things they are for centuries. I'm shocked. The Lord was called back and he left the earth. On May 31 to June 1, 2021, I was talking at midnight with Lord's and my negotiator; he told me that the Lord, when back, would like to come back home. The Lord and the others want me to call him back here. I need to find out what the stories are. When I was talking with my negotiator, I asked him, "What's going on with my condo at T. Tower in New York City?" He replied, "We are holding the deed because we want a piece of that condominium." Even after was given to me as a gift and it's in my name. M.T., at the White House, said to me, "Rich, that condo is in your name." They are afraid only of one thing: if I will move out from here, they will need to go back. They don't want to go where they came from; they are doing all kind of manipulations just to stay here. Just like she said to me, my number-one guardian angel at my office on November 12, 2012, "We came here to destroy you because you won't work with us." They still doing the same thing, but it's not easy to win with me and they know that. We have law here on earth; they don't want to respect that, but I will made them to respect because I'm the one with all the power and they know that.

I want to go back to our Pope F. after I send to him my early manuscript with all those pictures, drawings, and maps. I still didn't receive from him letter with any questions. Maybe I did the perfect job. I sent all proofs and explained everything clearly to him and maybe there'snothing left to ask for. I believe there is always something left to ask, and find out something untold.

On May 16, 2021, a golf ball hit our window and broke it while we were absent. This window crack created an image of me with side view.

On May 23, 2021, the second golf ball hit in the same spot, right in the center where that light spot it, and broke the second glass plate.

In the summer of 2016, there was a similar situation. A golf ball hit the window, and the crack made image of me with the side view of me. Yvona T., on February 15, 2017, took a picture of it after I did asked her to do so. That time I didn't take one. I thought one was enough.

I had been told by guardian angels that this car is the Lord's car.

I was told by my guardian angels that the car parked under this "pain" tree is the Lord's car. This car was parked there for about a year.

November 20, 2021

I would like to share with you my experiences. I don't think there is another person in this whole world who's has this kind of experiences like me. Once again, on November 19, 2021, while walking on golf course, I did spot man walking on grass on seven fairway. I thought to myself, That's the Lord. I made quick plan. I plan to meet with him after the seventh hole. He knew my plan, because he slowed down and we just met in spot I planned like always. I had short with him talk. At the end I asked him where he lived; he replied, "By Sue." I was try to think which one; he knew that and quickly added, "On Augusta Drive." Will be easy to see him on the camera. On the golf course they have cameras all over. He was walking by the golf club and they have cameras there. On November 19, 2021, there was a heavy frost on the grass; the average person wouldn't like to walk on it, but the Lord wanted to catch my attention and he walked on that frosty grass, and he did that?

On November 19, 2021, the Lord was walking toward that tree and golf cart path. Just like I planned. The Lord knew my plan because he slowed down, and we met there and we had short talk.

First time I met you, you were walking fast.

On November 19, 2021, the Lord was walking from that direction toward that tree and golf cart path. We met by the tree. The Lord was standing where that white dot is. I was standing on golf cart path.

The Lord was standing where that white dot is. I had been standing where the X is.

On November 19, 2021, the Lord and I met by this tree where that white dot is and I had with him short talk like always, and at the end of our conversation he said to me, "You go, because I won't like slow you down." From the

High Point, New Jersey
Fall of 2020

10-03-2020

On November 16, 2021, I was working all day long to complete my manuscript on which I had been working for over two years. I had been working very closely with my book coordinator, who was doing great job. I'm very grateful to her, for her help to make this book a very interesting to read. Without her, it would be hard for me to get to this point. On top of that, she was working for free. Not always are we collecting the praise right away; sometimes we will collect the praise later. Nicer and bigger, she won't be forgotten. On Tuesday I did go over my manuscript and everything was in the order. Then on Wednesday, after my coffee, something pushed me to check the manuscript. I noticed it was much thinner. I went page after page. What I discovered shocked me, I couldn't believe what I discovered. In the past I had all kind surprises, and not all of them were very pleasant. I had, in the past, had similar situations. But this one beat all those previous. When I got to page 49, I discover that sheet was missing. For now, we are type on one side of the sheet after page number 50. I found out there are more pages missing: Pages: 51, 52, 53, 55, 56, 57, and 58. Some pictures which were between those pages are missing too. Thanks to our God I have replacements. Also I have few copies of my book manuscript. Question number one: who stole a small part of my book manuscript? Why? I think I know why, because what I wrote there some people didn't like what I written on those pages; that's too bad, true is true. I did start my book with these words: "I would like to share my true, untold experiences with people of the world. I hope and I believe that with the God help everyone around the world will be able to read these true stories. About miracles that did happen and are still happening." When I wrote these words, people around the world will read this book; she, my guardian angel, knocked. I trust her. So I know why they stole those sheets from my manuscript. But I still don't know who did that dirty job. Yesterday all day I was upset; I like to keep my things uniform and in the right place. When something like this happens for me it is a disaster, because I don't know what those invisibles will do next. They are fighting for their lives. They are not that smart, they should know that I have copies all over. I don't think my guardian angels would do that. I had been thinking about those two in black suits with whom I met at Great Gorge, on February 13, 2016. They were elegant, stiff, and they looked unpleasant. President D.T. knows them, when Fox News Anchor L.I. asked him amid her interview, "Who's running J.B. campaign? President M.O?" President D.T. replied no; those people who are walk on streets in black suits. Now I know who scared my nephew to death after I did ask him for copies. I lost his family and my niece forever. MK told me a man came to her and scared her. Then he went to the Cardinal and he scared him, and he did the same with others. But I'm with all the power, and they know that. They are just like a mouse, walk far away from the cat. Or like those small dogs make a lot of noise because that's what they can do. They are doing what they're doing because they are afraid of me. And they right. They the ones who were to create the chaos with title search company. By put somebody unit number 61M there. They the ones who disabled my computer for nine days. My computer fixed itself, like always, and now works perfect. Always when I'm doing something on computer important and then don't like that, immediately they disable my computer. The was time my computer wasn't working for a couple weeks and then started to work again, without any repair. Yesterday I went to library to make copies to replace those missing then last night. I started to put my manuscript in the order. I pulled out a box with miscellaneous pictures. I needed to replace those missing. Yesterday I went through another shock. I pulled out from box all those pictures. I couldn't believe my own eyes, what I just discovered. Who put them there? Why did someone take those things and then place that in the box, underneath those pictures? I believe after I discovered the missing manuscript sheets and pictures, I was very mad, and I said that one who took these things will receive very harsh punishment and will go to Hell. I added that I want all that back. They decided to return my stuff and they did the right thing. But the damage was already done. That wasn't the first one, but I hope that's the last one. They are fixing everything just to prolong their life here. Once my guardian angel, Sophia's mother, was sitting next to me on sofa, and she was crying and said to me, "I don't want to die." That was in the summer of 2013. I believe she is here, since in 2002 the Lord once said to me "Why do these people like to be around you?" Because they like my lifestyle. They are living with me, next to me. Wherever I go, they are going with me.

November 9, 2021

I do have good guardian angels, and beside them are bad ones; we call them devils. They told me that they are angels too. Maybe they are right, they are doing their job too. I do have an example how hard, those bad ones working to keep me at present address and prevent me from moving out. At the sometime secure themselves where they are at present time. They love to be here around me (she just made one knock, which means yes). But that's not going to happen. Each time I am try to do something to improve my situation and when that is against their interest, they are send right away those two in black suits, white shirts, and black ties to prevent my action. In past they threaten people to whom I send letters and asked them to do anything for me but if that would be against their interest, right away they start working against me. My brother, my family members, and friends are reading Polish-American newspapers and when there were something written about me, they call me and share that with me. I did read one myself after my brother brought to me, Nowy Dzienik Polish news-paper publishing company, and I spoke with a person who works there. Her name was Justyna Ch. I asked her if they have newspapers from 2016 and 2017. She replied that they do. My next question was "Could you please find out those articles written about me, make copies and mail to me?" She replied "Yes, I will do that for you." To make it much easier for her, I gave to her all those important dates when I had press conferences or other important meetings. She asked me to give her couple of weeks to go through all those newspapers. After couple of weeks, she called me, and to my big surprise she said that she couldn't find any written articles about me or any of the stories I told to her. She was so nice and willing to help me. I knew what happened, one hundred percent. That one who visited M. Kelly and Cardinal D. and told him not to do what I did ask him to do, because if he would do that, after that would be the end of the world.

When he visited Kelly and told her if she would write the book with me, they would destroy her. She told me that at the White House on January 20, 2017, on Inauguration Day. Cardinal D. did the same on January 20, 2017, at the White House.

Kelly was so afraid after that threat that she didn't even call me or email me to inform me what had happened.

I believe that man also went to the office of Nowy Dziennik Polish newspaper, and threatened Justina C. the same way he did to Kelly.

She was so afraid after that threat that she didn't even call me or email me to inform me what had happen. What's going on? They have tremendous power over them over people they are threatening. Why are they doing what they are doing? They don't want me to have any proof in my hands and use to go after them and what's my but I have what do I need. If I would need more, I can get more. They know that if I will make one move, after that everything will be over for them; that's why they are doing anything to prevent me from that. Today is November 16, 2021. I am writing the last story in this book to share with you as much as possible. On November 5, 2021, I decided to call my attorney to ask him to get for me duplicate of the deed. I gave to him address of the property. It shouldn't be any problem to find that unit, which is in my name. There are only about 232 units in that tower. Sherlock Holmes would find it in no time. My attorney's advice to me that will cost $1,500 me for that search of the title. Also, he advised me that I could do it myself on computer from my home. I thanked him for his advice. I went to my computer. I found title search company. Next, I filled in the application with my name the address of the property; so far everything was good. When I wrote the New Jersey zip code, my computer didn't want to accept my whole zip code. My zip code is 07462. Each time I tried, it didn't want to accept that zero, and only started with 7462. I did so many times; immediately that zero disappear. I tried over and over, and after a number of tries, I succeeded. Next, I need to pay for my service, which was much less than $1,500 because it was only $87.95. I had been paying with my credit card; everything was going very smooth till I needed to put those three- digit numbers of back my credit card. Each time I wrote those 444, the first one immediately disappeared; it was left like that 44. After so many times of trying, finally I succeeded. Problems were not over yet. They did still fight for their lives. By now we know if I will move out, they will go back, but they don't want to. While I had been struggling with those three-digit numbers, Invisible wrote unit number right after the building number which was 721 building number. It added unit (fake) number 61M right after the building number. So the title search company instead searched for my unit and unit number they were supply with somebody's unit number and then searched for that unit title. Once again that invisible evil created chaos. On November 8, 2021, I called the title search company and I asked them how they were doing with the title search. That lady who was working there, replied it would be done that afternoon or the latest, tomorrow. I did check my emails same day and they didn't send anything to me yet. Then late afternoon I called the title search company and asked them if they have done the search of my title. She replied, yes, they did. It's successfully done. Yes, it was done, but not for my unit. They made title search for unit 61M. The unit number that invisible wrote in just after the building number. Which is not my unit number. So they had this property address! 721 61M 5th Ave New York City. Everything was correct except the unit number. I wrote so much about this matter, because this is living proof how some people come from above and use their powers to manipulate things for their own needs and benefit. Problem doesn't end up yet. Since then, my computer stopped working. In the past, when I did search on computer for something they didn't like me to do, they stopped my computer from working, and then after one week or longer to start working again. Today is November 17, 2021, and my computer is still in a state of disfunction since November 9, 2021. I believe my computer this time is gone for good, because this my action is grave, serious. In the past, I always got my things done, the way I did want and the way should be done. This time will be no exception. Here on earth, we have law and everyone must respect it.

I know President Joe Biden, since he was United States Senator from Delaware from 1973 to 2009. Joe Biden had always been supporting good programs and always voted for them. Joe Biden is a member of the Democratic Party, he previously served as the 47th vice president from 2009 to 2017 under President Barrack Obama. At the end of June 2016, President Barrack Obama and vice president, and members of President Obama's administration organized the historical meeting for me and Chancellor Angela Markel, Francois Holland "President of France'" president of Russia Vladimir Putin. Also, the President of the United States Barrack Obama was present, but sitting and listening while I had been debating. That debate took place on the Roosevelt Aircraft Carrier on the Virginia Coast. That meeting was very successful not only for the United States of American but for the whole world. President Joe Biden most of his life had have been serving our great nation, and the whole world. I had been always supporting Barrack Obama's administration, and now President Joe Biden and his administration. We are frequently exchanging letters and out opinions. I hope President Joe Biden will run for re-reelection in 2024, and successfully win.

THE WHITE HOUSE
WASHINGTON

December 13, 2021

Mr. Richard Langner
Vernon, New Jersey

Dear Mr. Langner,

Thank you for sending me your kind note of support and encouragement. I am humbled by the faith the American people have placed in Vice President Kamala Harris and me.

Our country faces many challenges, and the road we will travel together will be one of the most difficult in our history. It is time for all Americans to set aside their differences, try to understand one another, and strive to make the promise of a just, prosperous, and secure Nation a reality for everyone.

If we look ahead in our uniquely American way — restless, bold, and optimistic — and set our sights on the Nation we know we can be, we will meet this moment. I look forward to writing the next great chapter of the American story with you.

Sincerely,

Joe Biden